Mrs. Palmer R. Peterson

PASSION

PASSION

by Karl A. Olsson

Harper & Row, Publishers

NEW YORK, EVANSTON AND LONDON

FIRST EDITION

B-N

LIBRARY OF CONGRESS CATALOG CARD NUMBER: 63-10964

CONTENTS

PREFACE

Readers of my previous books may miss the comic turn. There is a time to laugh and a time to weep. The New Testament is joyous but not hilarious and in these pages we are together with people who must often meet in secret. We will have to forgive them their lack of jocularity. Most of them had to leave the laughter to the groundlings.

The first five chapters of this book were delivered in the School of Lent at the Fourth Presbyterian Church in Chicago during February and March, 1961; the sixth was a sermon preached in Rockefeller Memorial Chapel, at the University of Chicago, on July 22, 1962. Chapter seven has not been previously delivered or published.

Except where otherwise indicated, Scripture quotations are from the Revised Standard Version of the Bible.

KARL A. OLSSON

North Park College, Chicago

I. *Introduction: The Passion*

When the day of Pentecost had come, they were all together in one place. And suddenly a sound came from heaven like the rush of a mighty wind, and it filled all the house where they were sitting. And there appeared to them tongues as of fire, distributed and resting on each one of them. And they were all filled with the Holy Spirit and began to speak in other tongues, as the Spirit gave them utterance. ACTS 2:1-4

THE TITLE of our book has a deliberate ambiguity. *Passion,* as an English word, has not only many related but many diverse meanings. In its original religious significance passion meant the experience, the *undergoing,* of our Lord during the last moments of his life. In this context *passion* is the contrary of *action.* During the last hours he was delivered up into the hands of men. He was betrayed, bound, led, tried, humiliated, scourged, and finally crucified. It is possible to write the whole story in the passive voice. These were things *happening to* him.

There are classical analogues. In his *Poetics* Aristotle talks about the tragedy of undergoing. Reasonably good men are caught like birds in a snare. They struggle to extricate themselves, are bound tighter and tighter, and finally die in noble paralysis. This is *passio,* suffering.

Such undergoing is not the fate of weak men. Even in Greek tragedy the protagonist is not a man naturally incapable of action, but a man rendered incapable to act by the circumstances in which he finds himself. We recall the controversial inaction of Hamlet which leads at last to the utterance:

> Let us know,
> Our indiscretion sometime serves us well
> When our deep plots do pall; and that should learn us
> There's a divinity that shapes our ends,
> Rough-hew them how we will.

Hamlet is a man acted upon, a man undergoing and suffering, but his failure to act is not due to ineptness but to the curious enchantment of Elsinore: the something rotten in the state of Denmark.

Only the capacity to act meaningfully and with dimension renders a man fit to suffer. The men and women who groan and weep in the memorable tragedies are all people we must take seriously. They are not mice caught in a kitchen trap, but lions snarling in a pit.

The passion of Christ has an additional dimension. He entered the last grave moments on his own volition. He was not trapped or caught unawares. He did not fall, in the tragic sense, or succumb to a flaw in judgment. His followers were left with the curious impression that at any time he had the power to walk away from his captors. His passion was hence seen as a phase of a larger divine action.

We must be careful at this point, however, lest we fall into the error of those early heretics who robbed his passion of the quality of real undergoing. That he had the power to choose otherwise, does not mean that his was a totally free choice. Gethsemane shows that it was not. Being what he was, the passion followed as the only probable action. In this sense his character limited his freedom.

The passion of our Lord was, furthermore, something which he suffered above and beyond the hands of men. The dark and fatal element is not absent from Greek or even from modern tragedy. The tragic victim is struck down by more than daggers of steel. Christ's passion was a sacrifice in which he was the victim. He was offered up. The darkness and the forsakenness were not lessened by the concert between father and son. The passion was a true suffering, a going under.

The passion and its aftermath, the raising of Jesus, were in turn the causes of immense feeling. Pentecost was a tempest blown up by the fact of the passion and its revelation as truth. That the visitation of the Holy Ghost was seen as tongues of flame and heard as wind suggests the overwhelming character of the event. It was a revelation not only in the sense that it brought intellectual light but that it transported the followers of the Name into a new dimension of existence. Pentecost was true transport and, if we are careful of the word, ecstasy. It made the disciples seem drunk and a trifle mad.

In this sense the passion communicated passion. And this gives us another significance of the term. The early faith was enthusiastic. Gibbon, whose distrust of strong feeling is notorious, is probably right in charging the Christians with immoderate zeal. Gibbon's sympathies were with the cool and composed pagans who were forced to deal with these "lunatics"; from the eminence of his disdain he looked down with equal scorn upon the zeal of martyrs and of Methodists. Divinely inspired enthusiasm was nevertheless the tide which carried the church forward.

It was, if we can believe the historians, a turbulent age. And passionate, in the vulgar meaning of that term. For passion means not only the serious undergoing, the deep turmoil of spirit caused by the pressure of existence upon us; it may also mean the shudder of our senses, the excited riffling of the surface by a million shallow stimuli. It was that kind of age. An age working terribly hard to feel intensely by enlarging the area of sensitivity: more tastes, more smells, more spectacle, more pressures on the nerve endings, and also an increase in pleasurable emotion: transient sorrows and felicities. The excitement of the circus and arena—the whirl and clash of the chariots and the incredible bloodiness of gladiatorial shows—was not intended to move but to amuse, to crisp the surface of the summer seas.

It was the same with the theater. Augustine's delineation of its passions is applicable to the first as well as the fourth century:

> Stage-plays also carried me away, full of images of my miseries, and of fuel to my fire. Why is it, that man desires to be made sad, beholding doleful and tragical things, which yet himself would by no means suffer? yet he desires as a spectator to feel sorrow at them, and this very sorrow is his pleasure. What is this but a miserable madness? for a man is the more affected with these actions, the less free he is from such affections. . . .
>
> But I, miserable, then loved to grieve, and sought out what to grieve at, when in another's and that feigned and personated misery, that acting best pleased me, and attracted me the most vehemently, which drew tears from me. What marvel that an unhappy sheep, straying from Thy flock, and impatient of Thy keeping, I became infected with a foul disease? And hence the love of griefs; not such as should sink deep into me; for I loved not to suffer, what I loved to look on; but such as upon hearing their fictions should lightly scratch the surface; upon which, as on envenomed nails, followed inflamed swelling, impostumes, and a putrified sore. My life being such, was it life, O my God?[1]

A people so inflamed by the lust of the flesh and the lust of the eyes and the pride of life could not be expected to take kindly to the austere sectaries who gathered around the form and the meal of the Crucified. There were political reasons for distrusting the Christians, and the massive persecutions against them had the motivation of stamping out potentially subversive activity. But the conflagrations in places like Lyons, Smyrna, and Carthage were also fanned by more personal suspicions and hatreds. The Christians were kill-joys and the fury of which they were the victims was in part the fury of the aroused conscience. This is the meaning of the statement in the Apocalypse (11:10) that the martyrs had been "a torment to those who dwell on the earth."

In the calendarium of the church the word *passion* came to mean the death of the martyrs, and this became the regnant significance until the life and destiny of saints lost their primary claim on the attentions of men. In our present speech only the erudite think of passion as anything other than raw desire, usually sexual. Even the conviction of Milton that poetry should be "simple, sensuous, and passionate" affects us like the word "bowels" in the Authorized Version of the Bible.

It is nevertheless important for our time, whatever the semantics of the word, to be brought face to face once more with the strength of Christian passion. The contemporary church is in many ways emasculated. It has handed over the strong feelings to others and contents itself with a fluting amiability. This is true not only of the liturgical churches with their tepid rituals but of the so-called evangelical bodies where sober-suited clerics insulate their flocks from the savage realities. The reason that even church people read the Millers and the Mailers and buy *Lady Chatterley's Lover* at the corner drugstore is that they want something bloodier, angrier, rawer than the diet of friendly consociation.

I am not inveighing against liturgics so long as they are lifted up like banners in the midst of battle. (In Milan the antiphonal chant steeled the nerve of the orthodox against the physical assault of the Arians.) The Eucharist has significance as long as it is a true *viaticum* on life's hellish pilgrimage. I am not inveighing either against the nonliturgists so long as they retain some of the honest dourness of Knox and Bunyan, so long as they know how to fulminate sulphurously against the rot of our time.

We need passion in the church. And the source of it is supremely the passion of our Lord, not only perceived as the badly printed lines in a catechism but ground into our consciousness with the imaginative ferocity of the early Jesuits. If what our Lord suffered on the cross and what he suffers today in the midst of the anguish of sinful men is real, then the church must begin to *feel* it so that the pulses throb and the heart is lifted up in adoration. The church needs to feel. I am convinced it wants to feel. Around the country, priests are speaking with tongues and trembling under the burden of faith. How are we to interpret this except as a cry for passion?

To be brought back to the passion of our Lord is to find a reality which both invigorates and structures our enthusiasm. If through the medium of this little book we can be brought back to the cross and be made to stand with the primitive church at the source of its own passion, we may feel quickened within us that godly sorrow which works repentance not to be repented of.

II. *"By the hands of lawless men"*

Men of Israel, hear these words: Jesus of Nazareth, a man attested to you by God with mighty works and wonders and signs which God did through him in your midst, as you yourselves know—this Jesus, delivered up according to the definite plan and foreknowledge of God, you crucified and killed by the hands of lawless men. But God raised him up, having loosed the pangs of death, because it was not possible for him to be held by it.

ACTS 2:22-24

THERE IS now fairly general agreement that the Book of Acts, despite its relatively late date, reflects accurately the mood of the church during its earliest period. The speeches and sermons have an authentic flavor, and we may conclude that what we read of public utterance in the book reflects what the church thought about the Lord and his sufferings in the dawning minutes of its life. The brief passage from the sermon of the Apostle Peter at Pentecost, which heads the chapter, was addressed to Palestinian Jews as well as Jews of the Dispersion, who had gathered in Jerusalem for the holy days of the Passover and had remained on in the city. After claiming that the "mighty works of God" which had transpired during the past few weeks in the city, especially the stirring events of that day, were the fulfillment of the prophecy, Peter continues:

> This Jesus, delivered up according to the definite plan and foreknowledge of God, you crucified and killed by the hands of lawless men.

At least two things emerge from this *kerygma*—this proclamation of the apostle. The first is that the primitive church held the Jews responsible for the death of Christ. They crucified and killed Christ by conniving with the Romans in an act of ultimate lawlessness.

The second is that the lawless acts of men were comprehended within the larger mystery of God's plan and foreknowledge.

We must make clear at the outset why the view of the primitive church on the culpability of both Jews and Romans is important. We are painfully aware of the terrible struggle which the Jews have had to wage against the hatred of Christians who have charged Israel with being the murderer of Christ. No sensitive Christian can be anything but sickened over the many black chapters in the history of persecution written by the followers of Christ. Christians have hated, harried, tortured, and murdered Jews without number. They have enclosed them in ghettos; they have subjected them to the most amazing indignities; worst of all, they have shut their hearts against them. For over nineteen centuries Christians have forgotten that whatever may have been the sin of the Jerusalem Jews of the first century, our Lord prayed for them out of his final anguish, and that his prayer of forgiveness was echoed in the dying words of Stephen, "Lord, do not hold this sin against them."

But our awareness of the monstrousness of anti-Semitism and our shame for it cannot alter the record. If we are to give any credence to the testimony of the primitive church, we cannot support the unhistorical conclusion that it was the Romans alone and not the Jews who crucified Christ. The record of the Gospels and Acts, the testimony of the Epistles (some of which are very early in date), and the evidence of contemporary historians do not permit us to conclude that Pilate but not Herod, the Romans but not the Sanhedrin and the people, conspired in his death. The words of Acts 4 ring like a great bell:

> For truly in this city there were gathered together against thy holy servant Jesus, whom thou didst anoint, both Herod

> and Pontius Pilate, with the Gentiles and the peoples of Israel, to do whatever thy hand and thy plan had predestined to take place (Acts 4:27-28).

And the testimony of Paul written not twenty years after the crucifixion to the Christians of Thessalonica substantiates the testimony:

> For you, brethren, became imitators of the churches of God in Christ Jesus which are in Judea; for you suffered the same things from your countrymen as they did from the Jews, who killed both the Lord Jesus and the prophets, and drove us out, and displease God and oppose all men by hindering us from speaking to the Gentiles that they may be saved—so as always to fill up the measure of their sins. But God's wrath has come upon them at last! (1 Thessalonians 2:14-16)

I have adduced these terrible words not to arouse or justify any sick rage against Jews and Judaism. The primitive church did not testify to the complicity of the Jews and the Romans in the death of Christ because they hated either Jews or Romans. Nor did they do so, and this is singularly important, because they believed that either Jews or Romans were especially wicked. There is ample evidence in much of the New Testament literature that they thought nothing of the kind. On the contrary, what emerges in a careful reading of the New Testament is that the lawlessness which killed Christ, the terrifying hatred which raised its hand against the anointed of the Lord, was the lawlessness and hatred of good people—very good people indeed.

We need hardly be reminded that the leaders in the action against Christ were Jewish puritans, the party of the Pharisees, whose zeal for the application of the law to the minutiae of daily life was inspired by the loftiest ideals of purity and the most unswerving devotion to God. It was their conviction that a nation in which God was honored in all the trivia of life would be blessed and even emerge victorious in the uneven struggle with Rome. For them to be pious and scrupulous was hence to be patriotic; their salvation and the salvation of the land lived and died together.

It is easy to be cute about this kind of goodness. The Pharisee tithing anise and cumin and forgetting the weightier matters of the law; the Pharisee fussing with his phylactery and his prayer shawl; the Pharisee straining gnats and swallowing camels; the Pharisee keeping the Sabbath in holy stasis and blocking the violation of any of its minutest sanctities: the foot does not move, the eye does not wander, the belly does not beg for its food; the Pharisee reading and reading, praying and praying, weeping and weeping for the salvation of his little land—a few stinking rocks and sand hills and some brackish water—is he not ultimately laughable, this Pecksniff, this Ananias Wholesome, this unctuous Malvolio, be-laughed and be-spattered by the great Jonson and the great Shakespeare and the great Dickens and Goethe? Indeed he is pitiable and laughable.

But before we laugh and pity too readily, let us set him against his time and against ours. Set your Pharisee down in the streets of first-century Corinth with their bright-eyed lechery and their goaty lust. Let him stand, rocky lover of the Law that he is, in the midst of that effeminate, mincing crowd of pimps and panders: the nakedness; the rouged wantonness; the swooning coronets of passion; the lisp and the dandling;

the unguents, vials, aphrodisiacs, aromatics; the wines and the anodynes.

Or let him stand with the apostle in the crowded streets of Athens surrounded by a thousand dumb idols, carved, hammered, molten. Let him look out of his deep Semitic eyes at the obscenity and the despair. The chipping paint, the clumsy priapic symbolism, the pathetic lamp or food bowl consecrated by the tears of the suppliant and filthied by road-splash and every passing cur. And let him think, as he looks, upon the ineffable Name, upon the *tetragrammaton*, upon the Lord, the everlasting God, the Creator of the ends of the earth, who does not faint or grow weary.

It is easy to be cute about the morality of the Pharisees until we set it over against his time and against ours. The Pharisee in Hollywood; the Pharisee on Wall Street; the Pharisee in Miami Beach. What lessons in purity, unworldliness, and austerity could he not teach our time?

And if the Pharisees were good, so in their way were the Romans. They had the unhappy task of keeping a world from blowing apart, of binding the drying staves of the great international cask with hoops of steel. The legions were made up of soldiers, at that late date no longer the flower of Latin youth but mercenaries drawn from the fringes of the empire, a simple, direct crowd without much ideology or patriotic fervor or local loyalty, committed to doing their dirty job with as much dispatch as possible. The centurion says to his soldier, "Go," and he goes; "Restrain," and he restrains; "Kill," and he kills.

But in their hairy hands and their thick skulls the legionnaires carried the destiny of the empire. What safety there was, was due to them. On roads and bridges, on rivers and seas, in darkened cities, among rioting masses, the legions did their crude work until disorder and death overwhelmed them and the last brave cuirass rusted away among the ruins of the state.

Who killed Christ? The Jews did and so did the Romans, not because they were monsters of cruelty but because they were people, in some ways very good people. It is always the good people who kill Christ, and their lawlessness is not that of the jungle or the slum but the lawlessness of a good trying to make itself God. When our righteousness becomes our idol, we are prepared to make any bloody sacrifice for it.

Bishop Newbigin says it well:

> The more God's people strove to draw near to Him, the more deep was the gulf which separated them from Him. That is the tragedy of the Old Testament. And it reaches its climax in the Pharisees of the New Testament. These were the most zealous and energetic of the Jewish churchmen. They laboured unceasingly to bring the whole Jewish people under obedience to the Law of God. It was their aim to root out every trace of uncleanness in their lives and the life of their people. And yet it was these men who took the lead in the murder of Jesus. In that fact we see the nature of sin revealed. More than any other men, the Pharisees willed to escape from sin, but that very will drove them to the most terrible sin in the history of the world.[2]

The lawlessness which killed Christ is the rebellion which will pass through every repentance except the final one. The good man will repent of every sin except the sin of thinking himself good enough. It was the unceasing preaching of Jesus on excessive righteousness which struck at the root of Pharisaic pride and drove the Jews to the plot to put him out of the way. This becomes clear in the stark parable which, according to Mark, Jesus told his disciples on the eve of his passion. It is the parable of the vineyard let out to tenants, who, when the owner of the vineyard asks for some return on his investment, respond first by mistreating the owner's servants and finally by killing his boy:

> He had still one other, a beloved son; finally he sent him to them, saying, "They will respect my son." But those tenants said to one another, "This is the heir; come, let us kill him, and the inheritance will be ours." And they took him and killed him, and cast him out of the vineyard (Mark 12:6-8).

If we need further evidence, we can turn to the mournful example of Saul of Tarsus. There seems to have been no criminality in Saul except the criminality of goodness. There is something overwhelmingly beautiful and terrifying in his devotion to the religion of his fathers. Was there ever such a clean, sharp blade of loyalty? And yet with it in cold ferocity he hacked and hacked at the lowly followers of the Name until their blood bespattered him from head to foot.

We must hold life together. We must save our lives, our families, our institutions, our country. There is no way to do this except by being as good as it is possible to be. Righteousness exalts a nation. Law and government, as the apostle tells us, are not a terror to good works but to evil. The dusty legions marching down the long sad roads of empire, the majesty of Caesar in his palace of marble, all the thousands of minor planets, governors, procurators, sheriffs and bailiffs, taxgatherers and traffic officers—what are they but the agents of the

God of order and decency. There is much loose talk these days about the sins of respectability, and the solid citizen is held up to ridicule by every mangy beatnik and third-class existentialist. There is nothing of this in the Bible. The Bible has a mature attitude about anarchy. It knows enough about the chaos of lawlessness to respect even the bad emperors as long as they keep the creaking machinery of state functioning.

> The officer is God's servant for your protection. . . . The "power of the law" which is vested in every legitimate officer is no empty phrase. He is, in fact, divinely appointed to inflict God's punishment upon evil-doers. You should, therefore, obey the authorities, not simply because it is safest, but because it is the right thing to do. It is right, too, for you to pay taxes, for the civil authorities are appointed by God for the good purposes of public order and well-being. Give everyone his legitimate due, whether it be rates, or taxes, or reverence, or respect! (Romans 13:4-7, Phillips)

There have been periods in the history of the world when men have claimed Christ as an ultimate revolutionary. Apocalyptic Anabaptists, exophthalmic nihilists, gentle Fabians all have seen Jesus as an offbeat standard-bearer. Now it is certainly true that the mercy of Christ extends to all. Publicans and sinners become recipients of his grace. But he is not the Lord of Outlaws. He is not Robin Hood. There are in his treatment of those interesting Jews, Nicodemus and Joseph of Arimathea, and even of the Romans doing their job, courtesy and grace. And compassion. He knew the hard, thankless task which the rulers of this world are involved in. Hence Caesar is to be given his due. The emperor is to be honored. Law is to be seen as God's agent for good. But it is not to be worshiped. It is not God. Nothing is God but God.

But there are many idols. During the war a friend of mine was a chaplain in a prisoner-of-war camp to which thousands from Rommel's elite *Afrika Korps* were shipped. He tells of the young blond giants, the best of the *Herrenvolk*, the Eagle Scouts of the incredible empire. They were strong, healthy, and sullen. And hard. Their self-discipline was astounding and their resistance to democratizing propaganda was total. Nothing could bend or break them. But when they looked at a photograph of their Führer, their lips trembled and tears sprang to their eyes. He was not only their Reichsführer; he was their Messiah.

But let us not beat a dead horse. The Third Reich is dead, and the Führer's bones rest with those of his mad colleagues. But idolatry is not dead. On every hand we are tempted to raise up the creaturely to the level of the Creator, who is blessed forever. We idolize our children, our businesses, our institutions, our nation, our race, our way of life. They are good, but we want them to be divine. And we want to be divine. We want to remove ourselves from that judgment which keeps pursuing us like the Hound of Heaven. When God comes to us lowly and riding on the foal of an ass, we do him in.

How is it possible to live in the world and do our work without crucifying Christ afresh? How can we keep from idolizing the mortal and endowing the creaturely with infallibility?

There was once a man who had every reason to consider his cause absolutely just. He fought a battle for the oppressed, and he won the battle. It would have been understandable if in the pursuit of his high aims, he had developed a proud sufficiency. But it would be hard to find in the annals of power a man more keenly aware of his creatureliness. His favorite poem was a mournful lyric entitled "Oh! why should the spirit of mortal be proud?"

He had to make momentous decisions. In times of great national crisis, he had to depose and to demote as well as to promote and exalt. He was faced with a divided nation. While punishing the forces of rebellion, he had to assure them of his compassionate interest in them as well as of his stern rejection of their conduct. It was an impossible task, and Abraham Lincoln understood this. That is why he was, in his own way, a man of prayer. Lincoln was not a theologian. He was a statesman, forced to deal every day with the gray ambiguities of his office. But he did not want to crucify Christ afresh. He did not want to elevate his cause to the level of a divine infallibility. He did not want the South to be damned and rejected as if it were only evil. And so, bowed down by the weight of his cares, he prayed. And the meekness of his prayer breathes in almost everything that he did.

At the end of the Civil War, in 1865, when a lesser man might have expressed justifiable elation, Lincoln wrote:

> Neither party expected for the war, the magnitude or the duration which it has already attained. Neither anticipated that the cause of the conflict might cease with or even before the conflict itself should cease. Each looked for an easier triumph and a result less fundamental and astounding. Both read the same Bible, and pray to the same God; and each invokes His aid against the other. It may seem strange that any men should dare to ask a just God's assistance in wring-

> ing their bread from the sweat of other men's faces, but let us judge not that we be not judged. The prayers of both could not be answered; that of neither has been answered fully. The Almighty has His own purposes. "Woe to the world because of offenses! for it must needs be that offenses come; but woe to that man by whom the offense cometh." If we shall suppose that American slavery is one of those offenses which, in the providence of God, must needs come, but which, having continued through His appointed time, He now wills to remove, and that He gives to both North and South, this terrible war, as the woe due those by whom the offense came, shall we discern therein any departure from those divine attributes which the believers in a Living God always ascribe to Him? Fondly do we hope—fervently do we pray—that this mighty scourge of war may speedily pass away. Yet, if God will that it continue, until all the wealth piled by the bondsman's two hundred fifty years of unrequited toil shall be sunk, and until every drop of blood drawn with the lash shall be paid by another drawn with the sword, as was said three thousand years ago, so still it must be said "the judgments of the Lord are true and righteous altogether."[3]

We are citizens of a time which likes to absolutize its principles and deify its mandates. So horrible is the alternative to what we now have; so bleak are the prospects of a world ruled by the scourge of communism that we are becoming more and more wary of criticism. We don't want to be told of our sins. We want to be assured that because we are not Commies who work violence, we are above suspicion and judgment. What the Pharisees wanted of Jesus was the assurance that contrasted with the *goyim*, the bloody Romans and the decadent Greeks, they, the Pharisees, were an admirable lot: pure, austere, god-fearing, law-abiding, good. But our Lord preached not assurance but repentance. "Except ye be converted and become as little children." And they killed him.

It is near at hand for us who live in another time and under entirely different circumstances to dismiss the crucifixion of our Lord as the work of intolerance and fanatical national pride. It would be comforting to feel that Jews and Romans, *and only they*, crucified Christ. But to look long and hard at the first-century Jewish society is to see ourselves as a religious people not much more sensitive to the need for repentance than they. How great is our tolerance for the sort of earth-shaking demands which Christ would make of us today? How great is our receptivity to true repentance? How ready are we to sell all that we have, to renounce all that we cherish, and naked to follow the naked Christ? And isn't the alternative to this inner spiritual revolution, this earthquake of humiliation and repentance which Christ brings—isn't the alternative to this a discreet murder which will once and for all quiet his voice?

And so we also crucify the Lord of glory. We silence his voice. We join the lunacy around the cross and are fulfilled and tranquilized by that contorted body and that silent tongue. It is over. Praise whatever gods that be, we are rid of him.

And yet now at this very moment the greater mystery begins. For our lawlessness turns out to be his law. The murder of Christ is part of plan and foreknowledge, of destiny and predestiny. His death is no sooner finished, the last pulse quieted, the last spasm over, than the great counterpoint begins. Where sin abounds there does grace so much more abound.

The testimony of the primitive church was that Christ had been killed by the hands of lawless men, but inseparable from this truth was another, sometimes lost sight of—that this was done according to the definite plan and foreknowledge of God. The word recurs time and again throughout the new Testament texts:

> What God *foretold* by the mouth of all the prophets, that his Christ should suffer, he thus fulfilled (Acts 3:18).
>
> For truly in this city there were gathered together against thy holy servant Jesus, *whom thou didst anoint*, both Herod and Pontius Pilate, with the Gentiles and the peoples of Israel, to do *whatever thy hand and thy plan had predestined to take place* (Acts 4:27-28).
>
> Which of the prophets did not your fathers persecute? And they killed those who announced *beforehand* the coming of the Righteous One, whom you have now betrayed and murdered, you who received the law as delivered by angels and did not keep it (Acts 7:52-53).
>
> For those who live in Jerusalem and their rulers, because they did not recognize him nor understand the utterances of the prophets which are read every sabbath, *fulfilled these by condemning him* (Acts 13:27).

Strange and awesome is the testimony of the church on this point. Men perverted by frustration and rage had plotted their dirty work in Jerusalem. Pharisee and Sadducee forgot their enmity; scholar and politician joined hands; Herod, the fox, and Pilate, the pragmatist, put their heads together; soldiers in the barracks played their crude comedy with a reed and an old robe; thousands of people pushed and gaped on the Jerusalem cobbles; hammers were raised and driven against nails; human flesh quivered and blood ran—and behind and above all this conniving, heartlessness, and malice, all this indifference and coldness of heart and ultimate atheism, were the hand of God and the plan of God.

> O the depth of the riches and wisdom and knowledge of God! How unsearchable are his judgments and how inscrutable his ways! "For who has known the mind of the Lord. . . ?" (Romans 11:33-34)

The horror is not lightened. The sin is not lessened. Woe to him by whom the offense comes. But all the monstrous wickedness of men—and we need to think now of the very worst: the quantitative horror of thousands upon thousands of starved bodies crowded together in gas chambers and burial pits in Hitler's Germany; thousands upon thousands crushed by the heel of Russian power; and the qualitative horror, the sinfulness of sin—cannot overcome or frustrate the power, the wisdom, or the love of God. The stone which the builders rejected has become the head of the corner.

III. *"He who spared not his own son . . . ."*

What then shall we say to this? If God is for us, who is against us? He who did not spare his own Son but gave him up for us all, will he not also give us all things with him? Who shall bring any charge against God's elect? It is God who justifies; who is to condemn? Is it Christ Jesus, who died, yes, who was raised from the dead, who is at the right hand of God, who indeed intercedes for us? Who shall separate us from the love of Christ? Shall tribulation, or distress, or persecution, or famine, or nakedness, or peril, or sword? As it is written, "For thy sake we are being killed all the day long; we are regarded as sheep to be slaughtered." No, in all things we are more than conquerors through him who loved us. For I am sure that neither death, nor life, nor angels, nor principalities, nor things present, nor things to come, nor powers, nor height, nor depth, nor anything else in all creation, will be able to separate us from the love of God in Christ Jesus our Lord. ROMANS 8:31-39

SOMETHING has to be done. If people are like the people in Romans 1,

> filled with all manner of wickedness, evil, covetousness, malice. Full of envy, murder, strife, deceit, malignity . . . gossips, slanderers, haters of God, insolent, haughty, boastful, inventors of evil, disobedient to parents, foolish, faithless, heartless, ruthless.

If people are like that, something has to be done.

We would like to think better of ourselves. We would like a kindlier image. We may not be able to accept any longer the concept of the noble American which was current in the church a half-century ago: the idea that we *could* be Tennyson's Galahad.

> My good blade carves the casques of men,
> My tough lance thrusteth sure,
> My strength is as the strength of ten,
> Because my heart is pure.

Sinclair Lewis and T. S. Eliot helped to spoil that image. After *Main Street* and *Elmer Gantry* and *The Waste Land*, it was impossible to trust human virtue in the same way. After the Sunday supplement discussions of the ego and the id and Alfred Kinsey's reports, it was difficult to think of adult America as just grownup Boy Scouts and Campfire Girls.

But we would still prefer a kindlier image than that in Romans. Perhaps we are more like heroes in a Greek tragedy than like Paul's wicked men. Perhaps we are neither pre-eminently good nor bad but something in between. Won't it do to think of ourselves as morally middling people caught in an impasse? Half-noble souls suffering the results of a flaw in judgment? To see ourselves as the brooding and indecisive Hamlet, or as Othello presumed upon, or as the wrathful Lear? To believe that what we are is the outgrowth of confused causes? Certainly we have some share in the matter. But we were tempted or bewildered or under pressure. We did not intend the consequences. We did not mean for this to happen. Things got out of hand. We suffer from headaches. That day we were under too much sedation. Our vision is not acute. Other people do worse things and get by with them. We are seeing an analyst.

We would like a kindlier verdict about ourselves than the verdict of the Epistle to the Romans. Perhaps we are not much better than bugs avoiding for a few brief moments the heel which will crush us. We are only finite—looking out from bug-eyes and bug-souls upon a riddling world. We cannot understand life, we cannot cope with it; we act, but without responsibility. We realize that we are ignoble, sad, beat—O how beat!—but we are in the words of Richard Wright's "outsider" innocent. We are innocent bugs, hopping about in a grasshopper melancholy and waiting for Big Winter to come down with the Big Freeze.

We would like a kindlier verdict than that of the Word of God.

Let us set aside for the moment such vexed doctrines as original sin and total depravity. We shall not begin by saying that because we are Adam's seed, we are involved in evil. We shall not discredit such doctrines, for they have their place. But our true image of ourselves will not arise as a deduction from original sin but as a flash of insight gained by the testimony of the Word and the Spirit to us as persons.

However I came to be what I am, whether by heredity or unconscious wound or the hammering of my surroundings, this, in the light of the Word of God, is what I see myself to be. I am the man Paul describes in the twenty-one indictments. I may not be all twenty-one things at once, and many of these things I am not overtly or apparently. But I see myself in all of them. I see myself as fallen.

I have a friend in Europe who served for a time in the army of his country. He is not by nature lacking in kindliness and generosity. He is good to small children and dogs and is openhearted toward his friends. But he confesses to shamefulness in a trivial matter. When during his months of enforced service he received a package of goodies from home, he never shared them with anybody. He was not starving. He did not lack money to buy snacks. He yielded to an obscure need to make a pig of himself. With a sure stroke and with fine objectivity he used to sketch himself in the ludicrous army coat, three sizes too big, and in his melancholy German-style field cap, striding off through the snow and casting furtive looks around to see if he was observed. Then he would settle down on a stone or stump and open his precious package and stuff himself like a sad-faced ape monopolizing a banana in the corner of his cage.

It is not a very beautiful picture. My friend could have looked for reasons for doing what he did, but he was a Christian. He did not believe in subterfuge. He used to say quite bluntly, "I was despicable. I hate that image of myself."

And if people are like this and we are like this, then something has to be done.

I wonder if anyone at any time has given us a truer description of the disintegration of culture and of individual spirit than the apostle gives us in these few verses in Romans 1:

> For the wrath of God is revealed from heaven against all ungodliness and wickedness of men who by their wickedness suppress the truth. For what can be known about God is plain to them, because God has shown it to them. Ever since the creation of the world his invisible nature, namely, his eternal power and deity, has been clearly perceived in the things that have been made. So they are without excuse; for although they knew God they did not honor him as God or give thanks to him, but they became futile in their thinking and their senseless minds were darkened. Claiming to be wise, they became fools, and exchanged the glory of the immortal God for images resembling mortal man or birds or animals or reptiles. (Romans 1:18-23)

Everything is there in the briefest compass: God's revelation of himself and man's knowledge of that revelation; man's refusal to recognize God as God, his ingratitude, his turning in upon himself in futility, the darkening of his mind, and then all that follows: folly, confusion about the glory, idolatry, lust; and finally, in a carnival of horror, lust turning into perversion and inversion, the bestial and the ultimately shameless. It would not be incorrect to summarize the chapter simply as *what happens to men when they are left to themselves.*

I am aware of all the studies that have been made about innocent and happy people. *Growing up in New Guinea, Com-*

ing of Age in Samoa, Puberty among the Polynesians. The argument is often from romantic and sometimes from anti-Christian premises. It goes something like this. Primitive peoples are usually happy. Christian missionaries have made them unhappy by bringing in pants and Mother Hubbards and the doctrine of sin. If these children of nature had been left to themselves, they would have remained joyous and spontaneous.

I don't believe it. But even if it were possible to believe that peoples outside the law—that is, without a highly developed self-consciousness and mental irritability—are less prone than civilized people to rot, it is sure that self-consciousness breeds the decay the apostle talks about. The more self-conscious, and introspective, and knowing we become—in other words, the closer we come to formulating the human riddle correctly and seeing God as God—the more certain is our failure to recognize him and to be thankful. The two things—atheism and ingratitude—belong together: and they are the symptoms of brilliant and weary cultures.

From that high eminence of disdain, it is not far to all that follows. Pride leads to self-preoccupation and this to a sense of meaninglessness. From futility the road to confusion is short. Bereft of God and of the perception of eternal power and deity in creation because of him, and hungry for rest, we make gods of his creatures. The massive dignity of Egyptian sculpture, the ravishment of Greek marbles, the face and form of woman and man, the mystery of eagle, hawk, and owl, of bull and ape, of crocodile, cobra, asp, and lizard—what is this idolatry but evidence of man's darkened senses and the suppression of the truth?

And now the body too becomes a scene of confusion. It is

adored as the temple of the darkened spirit. It is festooned, sanctified, pampered, worried over. It is dressed in the costliest silks and drenched in the most exotic perfumes. Millions and millions of dollars are spent and millions of man-hours devoted to its beautification. Doctors are trained and hospitals erected and pharmaceutical houses organized and laboratories staffed to give the body its due. Wonderful and terrible is the despotism of the flesh!

But by a curious irony it is the same body which at the very height of its exaltation is plucked with the red-hot pincers of desire, scalded with acids, stupefied or overstimulated by drugs, bloated with food, and driven to the most perverse uses. It is violated, cuffed, dishonored, dirtied; it is whipped sleepless from place to place, the vehicle of a demonic spirit.

The closing scenes of Zola's *Nana* may be needlessly repulsive, but there is a hard scriptural truth in the way the glorious flesh of Nana is disfigured at last by the ravages of smallpox. All that darling goldenness which had so delighted the jaded appetite of the city is rashed over and cratered with pustules; all that heady fragrance is invaded with the odor of rot. To forget God is to give our bodies nothing but themselves. To adore the creature is to hand it over at last to its own weakness.

> Therefore God gave them up in the lusts of their hearts to impurity, to the dishonoring of their bodies among themselves, because they exchanged the truth about God for a lie and worshiped and served the creature rather than the Creator, who is blessed for ever! (Romans 1:24-25)

Such are men when they are left to themselves.

I don't know if we recognize ourselves in this horror. It is well if we do, for in this direction lies our salvation. But there are obstacles. There is the illusion that this acknowledgment of what we are without God is an attack on human dignity. "Glory to man in the highest, for man is the measure of things," wrote Swinburne. And it seemed in those days as if this were being kind to man. To free him from the graveclothes of Christian guilt and gloom, to garland him and anoint him, to set him down among clean-limbed men and maidens from some Attic frieze, to let him burn, in Pater's phrase, with a hard, gemlike flame.

But there is nothing so kind to man as to show him his true relationship to God: to show him fallen and falling, full of the sickness which the apostle describes, and yet beloved. To put a man face to face with himself is to put him face to face also with mercy.

Augustine writes with feeling:

> . . . but Thou, O Lord, didst turn me round towards myself, taking me from behind my back where I had placed me, unwilling to observe myself; and setting me before my face, that I might see how foul I was, how crooked and defiled, bespotted and ulcerous. And I beheld and stood aghast; and whither to flee from myself I found not. And if I sought to turn mine eye from off myself, Thou again didst set me over against myself, and thrustedst me before my eyes, that I might find out mine iniquity, and hate it. I had known it, but made as though I saw it not, winked at it, and forgot it.[4]

In this context we reread our Scripture:

> What then shall we say to this? If God is for us, who is against us? He who did not spare his own Son but gave him up for us all, will he not also give us all things with him?

He who did not spare his own Son.

There are atonement doctrines without number. This most precious word can easily explode in our hands. What does it mean that God offered up his Son for us? We cannot subscribe to a dogma which says something the Scriptures will not allow. God is not a wrathful and unloving Moloch who demands the blood of Christ as a means to expiate his anger. A father without fatherliness; a God without love. Nor on the other hand can we accept a view which says that Christ merely demonstrates or exemplifies divine charity. Three things must be involved in our salvation: a real unity in the godhead; real love; and a real sacrifice.

This is a doctrine which can easily become offensive, absurd, or obvious. The knife can be blunted; the great moment lost. In the sacrifice on Calvary the Father and the Son were one in desiring man's salvation. Kierkegaard insists that in the story of the sacrifice of Isaac we cannot believe anything less than that Abraham was God-fearing and pious, that he truly loved Isaac, and that he truly sacrificed him. The Mount Moriah story is a great if inadequate analogue to the Calvary story. In both there is a unity of intent between father and son, genuine love, and real sacrifice. The great Anselm of Canterbury has been repudiated by some because his atonement doctrine as stated in the *Cur Deus Homo* "bears the stamp of chivalry and of feudal customs." There is a certain unmodern love of clarification in Anselm. But Anselm is one with Paul and with Kierkegaard in understanding the mystery of Christ's passion as marked by unity, love, and sacrifice. He writes:

> he [Christ] had agreed with the Father and the Holy Spirit, that there was no other way to reveal to the world the height of his omnipotence than by his death. . . . For he preferred

> to suffer rather than that the human race should be lost; as if he were to say to the Father: "Since thou dost not desire the reconciliation of the world to take place in any other way, in this respect I see that thou desirest my death; let thy will, therefore, be done, that is, let my death take place, so that the world may be reconciled to thee."[5]

And finally:

> For that sentence: "God spared not his own son but gave him up for us all," means nothing more than that he did not rescue him.[6]

All the darkness of Christ's passion, all its ugliness, despair, and horror as well as its somber radiance are compressed into these words. *He did not rescue him. He offered him up.* In the first chapter of Romans the awesome phrase "God gave them up" is sounded again and again by the apostle. By an irony which lies at the heart of the passion the offering up of Christ is not unlike this. The relinquishing of rebellious man to his own designs is an act of divine wrath and of divine compassion; so is the offering up of Christ. It is the same God who proclaims his wrath against sin and who provides the divine sacrifice. It is the same God who offers up and who is offered up. And all of these mysterious facets are held together by our belief that Father and Son were one in intent, one in love, and one in the offering. The Father did not interfere with the passion. He did not force Christ to the cross, but once it was decided that he would go, he did not intervene. He did not rescue him.

The question has been made difficult by Freud. He seems to give us a picture of such hostility between fathers and sons that it is almost impossible to believe that love between them is anything but an artifice. Yet love is the foundation both of the Abraham-Isaac relationship and of that of Father and Son in the story of the passion. In both instances the act of obedience on the part of the son is an act of love. In both instances the burden laid upon the son is a burden of love.

Isaac is the son of promise. He is the future and the blessing not only of the droopy-eyed old man but of a people waiting to be born. "None was the child of promise in the sense that Isaac was for Abraham," writes Kierkegaard.[7] And it is possible by way of similitude to sense in Abraham's expectancy and joyous love for Isaac what was in the mind of the Father of our Lord.

We are helped by the most common experience. We know how it is for us. We have a son. He is our son. We have watched over his life from the earliest moments. We have seen him grow into boyhood and manhood. He is bright and clean, strong and yet curiously brittle. We feel the need to let him go and also to defend him. We do not want him to suffer. We remember with a stab of pain the occasions when he was hurt. We do not want this to happen again. We remember his rare tears. The brief convulsive sobs which rose out of an uncontrollable despair. We remember the knuckles dug into the eyes as if to hold back the shameful weeping. We don't want this to happen again. And yet this boy's destiny is suffering. This is what he must do not because we want it but because he chooses it. Do we begin to understand what was in the mind of Abraham on the way to Moriah? And in the mind of the Father of our Lord?

In the face of such circumstances, the most virtuous might well contemplate suicide. To be forced to give up what we love unto anguish may well bring us into such despair. If Abraham had committed suicide rather than agree to the sacrifice of Isaac, "he would have been admired by the world," writes Kierkegaard. ". . . But it is one thing to be admired, and another to be the guiding star which saves the anguished."[8]

This is the passion. The mystery of iniquity in us and the suffering charity of God. He spared not his own Son but offered him up for us all.

We ask why. Why did the Father offer up the Son for us? We are assured that he did it for a purpose. The purpose goes back to the very beginning of things. Even in the face of the Old Israel the New Israel may be discerned. God is calling out a new family in which Christ is the new Isaac, the son of promise, the guarantor of a blessed seed. And for those thus called in Christ and through Christ God will do what is needed. He will call, justify, glorify.

And with Christ he will give us all things. Phillips says that God will give us everything else that we need. But this can't be all that is meant. "All things" cannot mean merely enough to eat and drink or even an Old Testament blessing: fat cattle, loaded vines, oil in the beard, and six daughters-in-law heavy with child.

"All things with Christ" must have something to do with all that has been lost: creation caught in its wishful despair, in travail and in groaning; birds and creeping things, fish and cattle, microbes and the faint, far luminous smear on the horizon which is millions of universes bursting into life.

But more than this "all things with Christ" must mean the possibility of salvation for all those who repent: all the stony faces from the beginning of things which march toward us and away from us in Romans 1. Because of Christ all these proud, angry, rebellious, blinded, and perverse people can find a way back to peace across the burning marl of Hell. Because of Christ all of us lost ones may be enclosed in the ark of salvation and of intercession. And because of Christ, the charges and condemnations, the suits, accusations, libels; the unresolved guilts, anxieties, and morbidities; the scurf around the lips, the mossy tongue, the pounding head, the smarting eyes; the shame upon shame and the horror upon horror; the perversities, bestialities, cruelties, hatreds; the cold blood, the disdainful smile, the mocking laughter; the smacking of lips, the grunt, the belch, the lustful chuckle, the bored and impatient snort; the oath, the obscenity, the imprecation; the screaming quarrel, the shared scandal, the lip-licking lie, the monstrous exaggeration—all, all is over and done with, forever done with and forever over in the washing and sanctification of his most precious blood.

And nothing can now separate us from his love: tribulation, distress, persecution, famine, nakedness, peril, sword. No, in all these things we are more than conquerors through him who loves us. . . . Neither death, nor life, nor angels, nor principalities, nor things present nor things to come, nor powers, nor height, nor depth, nor anything else in all creation will be able to separate us from the love of God in Christ Jesus our Lord.

Something had to be done for us. It has been done for us. It is finished. So be it. Amen.

IV. *“When he was reviled, he reviled not again”*

Servants, be submissive to your masters with all respect, not only to the kind and gentle but also to the overbearing. For one is approved if, mindful of God, he endures pain while suffering unjustly. For what credit is it, if when you do wrong and are beaten for it you take it patiently? But if when you do right and suffer for it you take it patiently, you have God's approval. For to this you have been called, because Christ also suffered for you, leaving you an example, that you should follow in his steps. He committed no sin; no guile was found on his lips. When he was reviled, he did not revile in return; when he suffered, he did not threaten; but he trusted to him who judges justly. He himself bore our sins in his body on the tree, that we might die to sin and live to righteousness. By his wounds you have been healed. For you were straying like sheep, but have now returned to the Shepherd and Guardian of your souls.

I PETER 2:18-25

WHEN during the vast political upheavals a century ago a young revolutionary named Karl Marx wrote his *Communist Manifesto,* he was facing somewhat the same problem as the Apostle Peter eighteen centuries earlier. Marx wanted to perform an act of major social surgery. He wanted to extract the working class from its involvement in capitalist culture and make it a free, self-conscious instrument of the international revolution. He wanted British textile workers and German factory slaves and Belgian miners and Russian soldiers and French grisettes to stop thinking of themselves as Englishmen, Germans, Belgians, Russians, and Frenchmen. He wanted them to think of themselves as a new society, bound together not by flags and anthems and silly military memories but by a common misery, a common need, and a common hope. And he concluded his hot-eyed appeal to his comrades by the now immortal words, "Workers of the world, unite! You have nothing to lose but your chains."

The Apostle Peter, probably in Rome in the year 64, and writing to the scattered Christians in Asia Minor, sounds startlingly like Karl Marx many centuries later. For Peter, like Marx, was confronted with the death of a great culture and the coming to birth of a new. And like Marx, the great apostle was asking how this new society should be fashioned in order to do its work and fulfill its mission.

Now I am not drawing any simple parallels between the beliefs of the Christians and the Marxists. These beliefs are obviously light-years apart. And the differences in substance play their part in determining the different strategies employed by the two faiths. But in spite of this disparity in beliefs, the formal beginnings of the two groups are strikingly similar.

Both Peter and Marx were asking the question: How does a revolutionary group relate itself to its culture? Their answers seem not too dissimilar. A careful reading of First Peter suggests that for the apostle the church constituted an ark on the edge of the impending deluge. Christians were *exiles;* they were *holy* (hagios), that is, set apart; they were *chosen* and *destined* by God the Father and *sanctified;* they were *living stones* in a *spiritual house;* they were a *chosen race*, a *royal priesthood*, a *holy nation*, *God's own people;* they were *strangers* and *temporary residents* (Phillips); they were members of a *brotherhood* throughout the world.

What these terms suggest is the divorce of the first-century Christian community from its pagan culture. Christians are to be *in* the world but not *of* it. Christians are to think of themselves as a peculiar people, a band of pilgrims on their way to an eternal city. They are to form a ghetto, not in the sense that they perpetuate the physical isolation of the contemporary Jewish communities, but in the sense that they think of themselves as separate. Repentance, faith, baptism into Christ are intended to create a community which is peculiar. "How," writes the Apostle Paul, "can we who died to sin still live in it?" And Peter makes the divorce between the world and the church unmistakable in his letter:

> Our past life may have been good enough for pagan purposes, though it meant sensuality, lust, drunkenness, orgies, carousals and worshiping forbidden gods. Indeed your for-

> mer companions may think it very queer that you will no longer join with them in their riotous excesses, and accordingly say all sorts of unpleasant things about you. Don't worry: they are the ones who will have to explain their behavior before the one who is prepared to judge all men, whether living or dead (1 Peter 4:3-5, Phillips).

Such detachment is necessary if the new community is to attain self-consciousness and power. We need not labor the parallels with the early and prophetic Communists. They too thought of themselves as an eschatological community, an ark of salvation in the world deluge. The black hats, the badly pressed suits, the abundant mustaches, the melancholy faces, the burning eyes, the unyielding asceticism, the rejection of the temples and altars of the bourgeoisie, the plots, the strikes, the assassinations, the unhallowed liaisons between men and women—in how many thousands of ways real and mythical did not the first Marxists want to divorce themselves from their culture? Marx writes:

> In the conditions of the proletariat, those of old society at large are already virtually swamped. The proletarian is without property; his relation to his wife and children has no longer anything in common with the bourgeois family-relations; modern industrial labor, modern subjugation to capital, the same in England as in France, in America as in Germany, has stripped him of every trace of national character. Law, morality, religion, are to him so many bourgeois prejudices, behind which lurk in ambush just as many bourgeois interests. . . .
>
> The Communists are reproached with desiring to abolish countries and nationalities.
>
> The working men have no country. We cannot take away from them what they have not got.[9]

What is this but a secular re-enactment of the isolation and detachment of Christian communities throughout the long history of the church?

It is well for us to see the reality of this and to feel its power. The church which is merely one with its culture and which spends its energies in hallowing what is has forfeited its right to live. We may not agree with all the heresies and sects which have grown up within the church. There is something unpleasant and even ludicrous in these dissidents and dissenters. We feel the irrelevance of the Montanists with their bizarre doctrine of the Holy Ghost; the Albigensians refusing to eat eggs and milk and cheese because for them sin was in sexuality; the Anabaptists withdrawing themselves into somber isolation; the Puritans and their arguments for a joyless life; the Pentecostals relying upon visitations of religious feeling. We grow impatient with independent churches, free churches, separatists, critics, cranks, crackpots. We wonder why many of these people do not understand better than they do that today's sect is tomorrow's church and that no sect ever solves the problem of the generations. We plead for a sense of history and for an appreciation of the majestic progress through the centuries of the institutional church. We consign to oblivion all long-haired prophets, Christian radicals, holy existentialists, beatniks, iconoclasts, mountain goats, tract pushers, soapbox preachers—the whole wearying lot of fanatics and fools who cumber the ground and complicate our life.

We know the feeling, for some of us have lived a good part of our life on the fringe of Christian dissent. We are not unacquainted with religious frenzy, the hatred of the intellect and its culture, the hatred of the lust of the eye and the lust of the flesh and the pride of life, and the longing for the other world. We are not unfamiliar with the religious proletarian: his melancholy view of a world that is passing away and his childlike joy in the presence of the store-front *koinonia*—the brothers and sisters in the faith, their honesty, their immediacy, their love.

I have personally known and hated the ugliness of their meeting houses, the mediocrity and dullness of their preaching, the tinkle of their music, the desperate legalism of their life. I have known and hated the dourness of their holy men: their self-righteousness and their unresolved and impotent rages. I have known and hated the mousiness of their holy women, the sour smoke of their smothered feelings, their frightened goodness, the pinched quality of their sympathies. I have known and hated these things, and I understand the hatred of it which burns in James Joyce and in D. H. Lawrence.

But while we deplore all the diseases which isolation breeds in the church, we cannot escape its terrible necessity. The church is holy, it is set apart. If it whores after its culture, as has happened all too frequently in its history, it loses its ability to be the saving salt and sanctifies the horror in which it is immersed. Ezekiel gives us the wretched Old Testament parallel in the stories of Oholah and Oholibah (Ezekiel 23). The Roman church in South America, the Roman church in Italy and in Spain, the Orthodox church of Russia—all these are threadbare examples of what happens when the church no longer believes in its apartness. But we Protestant Americans need not be overpleased with ourselves. How clearly do we testify to that holiness, purity, modesty, and charity which should characterize the church? Must we not confess that we have followed the easier course of obliterating our uniqueness and identifying ourselves with the world? Must we not confess that in our desire to conform and in the fear of being thought different and eccentric we have adopted the camouflage of our world and live our Christian life, in the measure we live it at all, incognito? We are, as far as our time is concerned, plain-clothes men, indistinguishable and anonymous.

The church is not *of* the world. But the church is *in* the world. More than that, the church is *for* the world. This, I suspect, is the real difference between Christianity and Marxism. Peter is very insistent that the church must separate itself from the world. But he is equally insistent that Christians should serve in the world and pray for it. The isolation from the world is the isolation of love, not of hatred. Unlike the Marxists, whose strategy is to undermine the power of the state, Christians are to honor the emperor, obey the governor, submit to their employers, and have respect for everyone. They are to be model citizens and model workers, expressing their apartness not in fanatical hatreds and recriminations but in faithful witness to the truth, in modesty of life, and in loving service.

It is inevitable that the world hate them. The purity and shyness of the life of the primitive Christian, his refusal to join in the degraded and idolatrous rites of his neighbors, his refusal to be drunk with them, gluttonous, unchaste, ostentatious and proud, silly and abandoned, cruel and malicious—this refusal was bound to arouse the fury of his neighbor. There grew up within the Christian community the practice of wearing white rather than the many-colored and often bold garments of the pagans. They were hated for it. Christians also refused to attend gladiatorial combats and public spectacles, and were ridiculed. The Christians met at night; they shared in a common meal; they prayed, listened to the gospel, and sang the *carmen Christo,* the hymn to Christ. To their gathering came slaves, patricians, people of every class and color. They were hated for this practice. They were suspected by the government police of being subversive, and they were accused by their hostile neighbors of being immoral. They worshiped an ass's head; they murdered and ate infants; they put out the lights to indulge in the most shameless orgies. Thus ran the rumors.

Beyond the hatred and the rumors there was the public reviling. The Christians were not all proletarians, but many were. They worked in the factories, the mines, the shops, and the houses of the wealthy. Christians were different. Less irritable, less frivolous, less greedy; more honest, dependable, sober. It became an indoor sport to bait the Christians, to call them names—mealymouth, milquetoast, hypocrite, prude, prig, square—to blaspheme their Lord, to ridicule their faith, to accuse them of nameless acts, to bear false witness against them.

It would seem natural under these circumstances for the Christians to break off relations with their pagan neighbors, to withdraw into bitter isolation, and to bide the time for revenge. This was particularly true when reproach deepened into persecution, and in place after place through the connivance or indifference of the Roman magistrate Christians were harassed, tortured, and killed. The temptation to hate, to plot, and to kill in return was strong. Peter knows this. He knows how easy it is for the church to become perverted into an instrument of hatred. And he writes:

> After all, it is no credit to you if you are patient in bearing a punishment which you have richly deserved! But if you do your duty and are punished for it and can still accept it patiently, you are doing something worthwhile in God's sight. Indeed this is part of your calling (1 Peter 2:20-21, Phillips).

The real situation gleams through. Christians are being falsely accused and unjustly punished. They are being reviled and hated. In this situation Peter turns to the only source of light available to him: the life and death of our Lord. It is breathtaking to read his words in the fifth chapter of the Epistle, words sometimes glossed over but highly significant:

> Now may I who am myself an Elder say a word to you my fellow Elders? *I speak as one who actually saw Christ suffer* . . . (Phillips).

Speaking as one who saw Christ suffer, Peter directs the attention of the harassed church to the passion:

> Christ suffered for you and left you a personal example, and wants you to follow in his steps. He was guilty of no sin or the slightest prevarication. Yet when he was insulted he offered no insult in return. When he suffered he made no threats of revenge. He simply committed his cause to one who judges fairly (1 Peter 2:21-23, Phillips).

We have before us that fateful day in the spring of the year 29 or 30—some 35 years before this letter was written. Peter was then a relatively young man; now he is old, with the burden of the arduous years and the perplexing future upon him. But the events of the passion, although reinterpreted in the words of Isaiah 53, are as clear today as they were on that day when he saw his Lord die. And the heart of the passion, as far as Peter is concerned, is the sin-bearing of Christ.

> And he personally bore our sins in his own body on the cross, so that we might be dead to sin and be alive to all that is good. It was the suffering that he bore that has healed you (1 Peter 2:24, Phillips).

Because Christ was the sin-bearer, he took into himself with the resilience of the divine charity all that men could do to him. Peter must have remembered some of what he suffered: the insults at the hands of the Sanhedrin and the soldiers of the Praetorium; the jeers of the mob and its deceitful preference for Barabbas; the taunts under the cross, "If thou be the son of God"; the waspish ill humor of the robber; and all the physical horror of that day. But what he remembered most was the silence of his Lord. Wave after wave of hatred swept over him, and he opened not his mouth. He was silent with the silence of love. He was silent and did not revile because he did not want to break contact with the world for which he was being crucified. There are sullen silences and there are strategic silences. We are sometimes quiet because we are peeved and sometimes quiet because it may gain us a point. There is what may be called a public-relations silence. We are rarely silent because this is the best for all. But our Lord was silent out of grace. Toward him came the barrage of obscenity and hatred, the froth, the spittle, and the venom; toward him came a hail of stones and dirt and refuse, the sound of angry throats and rent garments, tufts of hair and beard from frenzied heads. And from him came only the great healing and reconciling silence of love.

Peter is saying to the church sorely tempted: Look, attend! This Christ died for you. Through him you are alive to all that's good. Through him you are healed. Now you are faced, as he was, with the reviling world. You must live his life and die his death. He suffered for you and left you an example that you should follow in his steps. You are to witness to him in the silence and healing of that forgiveness which is in you because of him.

May I say a word in closing about this great passage. It is so moving in what seems to be its heroic love that we are enraptured by it. "When he was reviled, he reviled not again." What a perfect summation of the meaning of the passion! It is indeed a great passage. But it is not a passage to which we can respond by any simple idealism. There is so much idealism in the world, so much talk, so much admiration, so many sympathetic tears, so many causes, petitions, posters, banners, editorials, protest meetings, lobbies. And there is so little forgiveness.

I should like to point out that Peter is not saying to the Christians in the dispersion, "Now, friends, let us consider the example of Jesus and try to be like him. Let us, like Jesus, try to be nice to our enemies." He is not saying that. He would have known the futility of saying that. What he does is to point first of all to the death of Christ. This is the premise on which the new life and the new love must rest. Christ suffered for you. Now, through that grace, you must be ready to accept what comes.

It is not impossible, like the Marxists, to separate ourselves from the world. It is not impossible, like them, to get ourselves hated by the world. But it is impossible to be apartists and to be hated and still to love and still to forgive. It is impossible to be Christians unless the crucified Christ lives in us. It is impossible to be related to the world in terms of love and forgiveness unless we bear about in the body the dying of the Lord Jesus. It is impossible to be silent in the face of reviling unless the Crucified is silent in us with the silence of love.

V. *"Jesus Christ and him crucified"*

When I came to you, brethren, I did not come proclaiming to you the testimony of God in lofty words or wisdom. For I decided to know nothing among you except Jesus Christ and him crucified. 1 CORINTHIANS 2:1-2

I have been crucified with Christ; it is no longer I who live, but Christ who lives in me; and the life I now live in the flesh I live by faith in the Son of God, who loved me and gave himself for me. GALATIANS 2:20

WE HAVE considered together a number of perspectives from which primitive Christians looked at the passion of our Lord. They saw the suffering and death of Christ as related to human wickedness, to the divine love and wisdom, and to their own behavior in the midst of fiery trial. They also saw it as that power which broke the shackles of sin and set men free. It is the passion in this last sense, that is, as justifying and sanctifying grace, which we now want to consider.

Some time in the year 50 of our era the Apostle Paul came to the city of Corinth in the Greek province of Achaia. The city was a large and busy metropolis, capital of its province and straddling the isthmus which joins the Peloponnesus to the Greek mainland. Across this narrow neck of land ships from both east and west were dragged to avoid the treachery of the seas and to shorten the voyage from the Aegean to the Adriatic. While the ships were in portage, crews and passengers poured into the city, adding to the already cosmopolitan population an unending stream of novelties from Alexandria and Antioch, from Carthage, Ephesus, and Rome.

Corinth was a religious city in the sense that most of its energies were devoted to sanctifying and celebrating the mysteries of the flesh. The city was dominated by a mountain citadel called the Acrocorinth in which had been built an elaborate temple to Aphrodite. Aphrodite was the goddess of love, and there flourished within the temple courts as well as in the city proper a brisk trade in human favors. Beyond this obvious type of idolatry, there was a more subtle form of devotion to the life of the world. There were in Corinth many temple guilds, each devoted to its special craft and its patron god or goddess. It was customary for the members of a guild to sacrifice to their patron and to eat a sacred meal in honor of the god within the temple precincts. These meals were convivial occasions much like a Kiwanis lunch, and as goldsmiths, potters, fullers, and vintners, Christians were expected to participate.

The Corinthians were a people of hot, quick passions and heedless loyalties. Their instability of feeling expressed itself in many ways. They formed factions and cliques; they alternated between the abandoned sexual life of the city and extreme austerity; they devoted themselves to ecstasy: trances, speaking with tongues, prophetic utterance, healing; they yielded easily to heresy, questioning the resurrection of the dead and the authority of Paul and giving a magic significance to baptism and the eucharist; they needed considerable urging in the stewardship of gifts; they were proud and power hungry and too much impressed with intellectual brilliance and especially with eloquence. Above all, they seem to have been deficient in love. They had not yet learned the mystery of the cross or embraced its power.

Paul stayed in Corinth for eighteen months, ministering first to the Jews, and when he was rejected by them, to the Gentiles. From Corinth he went briefly across to Ephesus and then back to Jerusalem. Later he returned to Ephesus for an extended visit, and from that city came the Corinthian correspondence which is preserved in the New Testament.

Paul's letters to the Corinthians are amazingly alive. Even today after nineteen centuries they are fresh as the morning's newspaper. It is impossible to read them without realizing that Paul is addressing real people with real problems. They are human beings who have passed through a life-shaking, life-transforming experience. They have been given a new life; they are made over; they are filled with the mysterious power of the heavenlies. Paul writes:

> Have you forgotten that the kingdom of God will never belong to the wicked? Don't be under any illusion—neither the impure, the idolater or the adulterer; neither the effeminate, the pervert or the thief; neither the swindler, the drunkard, the foul-mouthed or the rapacious shall have any share in the kingdom of God. And such men . . . were some of you! (1 Corinthians 6:11, Phillips)

Such were some of you.

When the Christian faith crossed over from Judaism to the Gentile world, it confronted a host of new situations. The Jewish people, especially those who remained true to the synagogue and its traditions, were outwardly moral. Like the Christians they kept themselves largely unspotted from the pagan world. In fact, much of the fury with which they opposed the preaching of Paul can be traced to their disappointment in his message. They expected him to take their part. But instead of commending them for their moral goodness, he called them to inner repentance and new faith.

With the pagans the situation was quite different. The old pagan morality which is reflected in the Greek historians of an earlier period was now corroded under the pressures of a city civilization. The virtuous Baucis and Philemon of Greek legend may still have been living in domestic purity in some upland village, far from the clamor of Corinth, but in Corinth things were far from pure. When Paul, after concluding the catalogue of vices, says "Such were some of you," he means this in a literal sense. The Corinthians had been people like that. In terms of Jewish morality, they had been untouchable.

We feel embarrassed by this. It is difficult for us in the evangelical Protestant tradition to focus very long on the Corinthians as pagans. We feel the same revulsion as did English evangelicals when William Booth began his work among the dregs of English society. We are nauseated by the shamelessness of it, by its physicality, by its vulgarity. We say, a bit naïvely, "How can people be like that?" We ask with Desdemona in *Othello*, "Wouldst thou do such a deed [i.e., commit adultery] for the whole world?"

And yet it is well for us, before we rush on into a more pleasant landscape, to look steadily at what the apostle is saying. *Such were some of you.*

Some of the Corinthians had been the worst. They had been the Magdalens and Messalinas, the Becky Sharps and Emma Bovarys and Grushenkas, the Smerdyakovs and Raskolnikovs. They had sensed within them the itch, the giddiness, the hilarity, the abandonment, the drained exhaustion, the stupor, and the sterility of their wants. With candor Paul focuses on the underside of Corinthian life. We see before us the same lurid scenes which Dante gives us in the *Inferno*, and James Joyce in the nightmarish visit of Leopold Bloom to the night spots of Dublin. This is the street of the thief and the swindler, the meretrix and the monster. All is for the slaughter of souls. We remember the words of Jesus: "The thief comes only to steal and kill and destroy." Like the pale, grubby creatures we disturb when we turn over a rock, these half-humans peer out at us from the shadows of Corinth. All is false. All is stage scenery, wild lighting: purples, oranges, vermillions; all is cosmetic: the wide-staring bloodiness of the mouth, the chalked cheeks, the eyes streaked with kohl, the hennaed wig. All is to allure, to seduce, to bind, and to slay. The gaming tables with their false promise, the whisper of the con man, the little intimate taverns with the gurgle of the wineskins, the fragrance of garland and incense from softly lighted doorways.

Such were some of you. But a miracle had happened. The world had been made over and men reborn.

> *And such were some of you.* But you were washed, you were sanctified, you were justified in the name of the Lord Jesus Christ and in the Spirit of our God.

Let us not for a moment worry about words. Sanctification and justification are honorable words, enshrined forever in millions of theological pages. Let us leave the theologians to deal with them. Let us turn instead to the homely human fact which confronts us in Paul's letter. The Corinthians had been dirty. One day they had been offered cleansing. The offer had come in words uttered by an insignificant man in the house of Titius Justus next to the synagogue. It may have been in the morning, when some of them were dragging themselves home from a night of partying, that they saw the crowd in front of the house and pushed their way in. Or it may have been at night when they were drawn to see what went on in the house and found the volcanic Jew from Tarsus in the midst of dock hands and pottery slaves, patricians and temple women. They had listened, had begun to feel ashamed, had questioned, had argued with themselves and later with others. They had looked around and had seen the beginnings of something in the faces. They had seen something in the face of the Jew and the beginnings of something in the hard faces of the women. Under the rouge and the chalk and the blackened eyelashes the frost was breaking up. And they had gone in and out not once but many times. They had returned to the gurgling of the wineskins and to the street of shame. They had been more intense and angrier and wilder in their sinning. And they had come back meekly to the house of Justus and the proclamation of the Jew. Then one day in a spasm of contrition they had cast themselves into the abyss of faith. They had let go of the edge and had hurtled down a thousand feet into the sea. And the great salt sea had washed over them, burning and scrubbing them, washing and blessing. And such were some of you, but you were washed, you were sanctified, you were justified in the name of the Lord Jesus and in the Spirit of our God.

Such were some of you, but you were washed . . . sanctified . . . justified. You were dirty; now you are clean. You were unholy; now you are holy. This in essence is salvation. Men are brought out of darkness into light. Men are brought out of sickness into health and out of death into bursting green and blossom and fruit. "You he made alive," says the apostle. How does it come about?

It goes back to the cross. In the cross God launched his counterattack against evil. From the death of Christ a tide of salvation and new life moves out across the world. All human efforts to save and bless: the moral power of the Jews and the intellectual power of the Greeks, all these ingenious systems so deep, so well meant, so full of good feeling and kindliness —what are they but little gusts of wind playing in the rigging of the beached and impotent ship of our existence? We must be right, or made right. We must be just, or made just. Everything in us cries out for cleansing and for righteousness.

> Men and brethren, what shall we do? . . . Sirs, what must I do to be saved? . . . Lord, that I may receive my sight! . . . Lord, be merciful unto me, a sinner. . . . Remember me when thou comest into thy kingdom. . . . Father, I have sinned against heaven and in thy sight and am no more worthy to be called thy son. . . . Against thee, thee only have I sinned. . . . My sin is greater than I can bear.

The words rise like a chorus from the throats of men and women in all ages and in all places.

And in answer to them there is the word of the apostle to his Corinthian converts, "I decided to know nothing among you except Jesus Christ and him crucified." His life poured out for us is our life, our baptism, our cup of blessing. Jesus Christ and him crucified.

I have a friend who spends time helping people with their feelings. For a man who deals constantly with human unhappiness, he is a singularly free and joyous person. It is his testimony after seeing and hearing the troubles of hundreds of people that either we accept the atonement of Christ or we repeat it. That is, either we believe that the thing which happened on Calvary is adequate for us or we proceed to do it over again in our own strength. All around us, my friend tells me, there are people who are punishing themselves in their effort to atone for their own sins and for the sins of others. They sicken, or smoulder with mysterious rages, or impose terrible burdens on themselves; they wear themselves out in fruitless and joyless activity.

Martin Luther is our classic example of a man who did not believe that the atonement of Christ was good enough for him. He not only beat himself externally until the blood ran; he lacerated himself inwardly with the barbs and thorns of a thousand questions. He did not dare to be free or to be joyous in the assurance that Christ had died for him. He felt that he must continue to do the work of Calvary over again, carrying upon his back the unexpiated sins of the world.

It was only when Luther began to read the writings of the Apostle Paul—the great message of justification by faith alone, faith in the work of Christ on the cross on our behalf—that an end came to his burning quest and he found his way into peace.

The story of John Wesley is no less familiar. John and Charles Wesley made a name for themselves at Oxford in the 1730s. They were sober and methodical Christians. Soon a group of young men with the Wesleys at the center formed the "Holy Club," which devoted itself to studying the New Testament in Greek as well as religious classics. It fostered spiritual discipline through fasting, regular communions, and prayer. The program of these people is quite above praise. They were not hypocrites or psalm singers. They were intelligent, alert, and devoted men: the kind of men who, when we find them in a theological seminary, gladden us with their promise. When in October, 1735, Charles and John Wesley set sail as missionaries to Georgia, they were sustained by the interest and prayers of many devout souls in England.

We need to read the *Journal* of John Wesley in order to believe what followed. On shipboard, John arose every morning at four and retired at nine in the evening. Of his seventeen waking hours he spent eleven in religious exercises. He prayed mightily, he read his Bible, he carried on edifying conversations with his fellow passengers, he studied the German language, he preached.

But he noticed with dismay that he was not so secure as his Moravian friends aboard ship. When a severe storm broke out, he was terrified, not so much by the prospects of death as of a judgment for which he was not prepared. The story of his three-year failure in Georgia is too well known to need repeating. He returned to England in 1738, a frustrated man. In terms of every outward appearance John Wesley was a model Christian. But inwardly he was cold and dead, filled with self-loathing and the need to punish himself for his great fiasco.

It is significant that John Wesley, the austere evangelical monk, should encounter at that critical moment the words of another monk miraculously healed. He went back to his Moravian friends, circling around them with burning eyes and a hollow chest. He talked to Peter Böhler, and then on May 24, 1738, he went to the Moravian meeting at Aldersgate. He was a man trying to repeat the atonement, trying to do Christ's work over again. Then,

> About a quarter before nine, while he [the leader of the meeting] was describing the change which God works in the heart through faith in Christ, I felt my heart strangely warmed. I felt I did trust in Christ, Christ alone for salvation; and an assurance was given me that He had taken away my sins, even mine, and saved me from the law of sin and death.[10]

It was the old story over again: Saul on the road to Damascus, Augustine under the orchard tree in Milan, Luther in his tower. The great, the simple, the terribly simple and terribly great step had been taken from death into life. And such were some of you. But you were washed, you were sanctified, you were justified in the name of the Lord Jesus Christ and in the Spirit of our God.

We either accept the atonement or we repeat it. But having accepted it, what do we do next? If it is a heresy in the church that man can achieve salvation in his own strength and that he need not concern himself with a justifying encounter, it is equally heretical to believe that it is a one-time experience. Nothing in this life saves us permanently: not baptism or confirmation or decision-making or even ministerial ordination. To confront grace is to be plunged into a dynamic experience which ebbs and flows, waxes and wanes. We are reminded of this by the two great sacraments or ordinances of the church. In baptism we celebrate cleansing and justifying grace; in holy communion we are nourished as the body is nourished from day to day and hour to hour. This is the meaning of Paul's word in Galatians:

> I am crucified with Christ: nevertheless I live; yet not I, but Christ liveth in me: and the life which I now live in the flesh I live by the faith of the Son of God, who loved me, and gave himself for me.

Sanctification, that is, making life holy, was for the Apostle Paul the work of the crucified and risen Lord within himself. Whatever there was of victory over the powers of evil within him came about because he was joined in faith with the Victorious Christ. In a way much too realistic to describe, Paul believed that he carried about with him the dying of the Lord Jesus. This is what he means by the fellowship of suffering and by filling up the sufferings of Christ. When Paul suffered, as he did many times, it was not Paul repeating Calvary or doing Christ's work over again. It was Christ suffering and triumphing within him. Christ was in the best sense Paul's alter ego, his other I, as well as his own I, if by this we mean not the loss of Paul as a person but his transformation into a new creature. The same strong conviction that the risen Lord lives within the church and in the hearts of its people is reflected in the words of John:

> Little children, you are of God, and have overcome them [that is, the spirit of antichrist]; for he who is in you is greater than he who is in the world (1 John 4:4).

There is a curious story in the martyrology of Carthage about the death in the arena of Perpetua, a noble matron, and Felicitas, a slave girl. Felicitas was pregnant when she was imprisoned, and she gave birth to a child only a few days before the exhibition was scheduled for the arena. During the travail of birth some of the jailers who stood by taunted her:

> You who are in such suffering now, what will you do when you are thrown to the beasts? . . .

Felicitas replied:

> Now it is I that suffer what I suffer; but then there will be Another in me who will suffer for me, because I also am about to suffer for Him.[11]

A few days later she was gored to death by a wild cow in the presence of jeering thousands who while the blood flowed shouted, "Saved and washed, saved and washed."

It is impossible for us to understand fully the brutality of the scene. What we do know is that the cries of the bloodthirsty crowd became an ironic testimony to the sanctification of those who suffered. Because Christ was truly suffering in them and for them, his blood mingled with theirs in an act of ultimate cleansing and sanctification. The words of a slave girl became the rallying cry of a besieged church, "There will be Another in me who will suffer for me."

But, we may ask, what does this kind of sanctification have to do with us, who take buses to the office, worry about down payments and the schooling of our children and perhaps about our blood pressure, and live for the most part lives without martyrdom or even the mildest harassment because of our faith? What does Paul, the apostle, or Felicitas, the Carthaginian martyr, have to do with us? What's Hecuba to us or we to Hecuba that we should mourn for her?

These are good questions, and if we were only two-dimensional people who could exist like flat flounders at the surface of life, we would not need to worry about being anything but sociable fish on their way to the ultimate fish fry. But we are creatures of depth, and what happens far below the surface within us is more important than what happens on the surface. We know this almost instinctively. Graham Greene in *Brighton Rock* sketches an old Catholic woman, sunk in degradation and misery, a repulsive mountain of dying flesh, who nevertheless clings to her crucifix and mumbles her prayers. The cross and the prayers define her much better than the perishing flesh. The old questions: What must I do to be saved? and How may I please God? are much more meaningful for us than the tax structure or national defense.

"Jesus Christ and him crucified"—the fact and the testimony are evidence of God's relentless grace. He has made us for himself and he wants us. He has made us for himself and we remain restless and miserable until he has found us and has begun his work in us. The cross is his call and his assurance. He will wash us, he will sanctify, he will justify. He will chasten, test, purge, and humble. He will weigh and judge, question and insist. All is his mercy who having begun a good work in us will complete it until the day of Christ.

C. S. Lewis gives us a modern version of the old story in *Surprised by Joy:*

> You must picture me alone in that room in Magdalen, night after night, feeling, whenever my mind lifted even for a second from my work, the steady, unrelenting approach of Him whom I so earnestly desired not to meet. That which I greatly feared had at last come upon me. In the Trinity Term of 1929 I gave in, and admitted that God was God, and knelt and prayed: perhaps, that night, the most dejected and reluctant convert in all England. I did not then see what is now the most shining and obvious thing; the Divine humility which will accept a convert even on such terms. The Prodigal Son at least walked home on his own feet. But who can duly adore that Love which will open the high gates to a prodigal who is brought in kicking, struggling, resentful, and darting his eyes in every direction for a chance of escape? The words *compelle intrare*, compel them to come in, have been so abused by wicked men that we shudder at them; but, properly understood, they plumb the depth of the Divine mercy. The hardness of God is kinder than the softness of men, and His compulsion is our liberation.[12]

The language is that of a cultivated Oxford don, but the experience of grace, the mystery of the Crucified, is the same for him as for Saul of Tarsus and the dejected Anglican John Wesley, and us all. "I determined to know nothing among you except *Jesus Christ and Him crucified.*" "I am crucified with Christ." "Christ lives in me."

> We think that Paradise and Calvary,
> Christ's cross, and Adam's tree, stood in one place;
> Look, Lord, and find both Adams met in me;
> As the first Adam's sweat surrounds my face,
> May the last Adam's blood my soul embrace.
>
> So, in his purple wrapped receive me Lord,
> By these his thorns give me his other crown;
> And as to other souls, I preached thy word,
> Be this my text, my sermon to my own,
> Therefore that he may raise the Lord throws down.[13]

VI. *"Outside the camp"*

We have an altar from which those who serve the tent have no right to eat. For the bodies of those animals whose blood is brought into the sanctuary by the high priest as a sacrifice for sin are burned outside the camp. So Jesus also suffered outside the gate in order to sanctify the people through his own blood. Therefore let us go forth to him outside the camp, bearing abuse for him. For here we have no lasting city, but we seek the city which is to come. Through him then let us continually offer up a sacrifice of praise to God, that is, the fruit of lips that acknowledge his name. HEBREWS 13:10-15

I HAVE WANTED to include in the witness of the most ancient church to the crucifixion of our Lord also a word from the Epistle to the Jewish Christians, commonly called the Epistle to the Hebrews. It is a most interesting letter. It was for many centuries ascribed to the Apostle Paul, and the King James Bible retains the ascription. But it cannot be Paul's unless we assume his adoption of a style and theology entirely different from that in his other letters. Even if the writer is not Paul, however, Hebrews is a powerful testimony to the Pauline truth of the importance of Jesus Christ and him crucified.

It is impossible here to do any kind of justice to the epistle in its entirety. The heart of it is the fulfillment of all things in Christ, and the essence of this fulfillment is the atoning work of Christ on the cross. In Christ the elaborate sacrificial cultus of the Jewish faith: the tabernacle, the altar, the high priest, the sacrificial animal, the sacrifice and the sprinkling of blood and even the holy and shameful residue—so holy and so shameful that it could not be eaten by the priests but must be carried outside the camp and burned—in Christ all, all is fulfilled.

Christ is tabernacle, altar, priest, and sacrificial animal. The crucifixion is the sacrificial act and the sprinkling and the atonement. And Christ's death outside the gate is a solemn re-enactment of the bringing out of these animals slain yearly in the ritual of atonement. The meaning of their shame and their sanctity is buried in the deeps of antiquity. Were the slain animals so tabooed because they carried away the ritual sins of the people? Were they, in other words, so saturated by sin that they would have killed anyone eating them? Or were they ingodded, impregnated with the divine glory? And was this the reason for their hurried and secret transport to the burning pits outside the camp? We don't know. All we know is that when the writer to the Hebrews surveyed the meaning of the cross, he saw in it the mystery of fulfillment. All that was formerly done day after day and year after year in tabernacle and temple has now been done once and for all by Christ as the perfect priest and victim. The earthly has once and for all been replaced by the heavenly; the seen by the unseen. Christians no longer come to things that can be touched or seen or heard. They no longer see and adore the processions of doves and heifers and lambs into the shambles and the ritual slaughter by the priests. There is no longer the bleat of the dying, the reek of blood, the curl of altar smoke. All this is over and done with. Because of Christ Christians can leave behind the old order and embrace the new. Our writer makes this clear:

> You have not had to approach things which your senses could experience as they did in the old days—flaming fire, black darkness, rushing wind and out of it a trumpet blast, a voice speaking human words. . . . No, you have been allowed to approach the true Mount Zion, the City of the living God, the heavenly Jerusalem. You have drawn near to the countless angelic army, the great assembly of Heaven and the Church of the first-born whose names are written above. You have drawn near to God, the Judge of all, to the souls of good men made perfect, and to Jesus, mediator of a new agreement, to the cleansing of blood which tells a better

story than the age-old sacrifice of Abel (Hebrews 12:18-24, Phillips).

It is in this context we see the special exhortation to first-century Christians which we want to consider together:

> Therefore let us go forth to him outside the camp, bearing abuse for him. For here we have no lasting city, but we seek the city which is to come.

Let us begin with a very simple question. What does it mean that Jesus suffered *outside* the gate and that we are to go to him *outside* the camp and to bear his disgrace?

It is clear that for the writer of the epistle the death of Christ outside the wall re-enacted the ritual of rejection whereby the animals used in the sacrifice of atonement were destroyed outside the camp. Christ's death outside the gate is the perfection and the putting to an end of the sacrifice and the rejection. We share in this sacrifice of our Lord and are sanctified, that is, set apart, by it.

But if we are sanctified by Christ's death outside the gate, we must also be prepared to go out to him—and here the figure changes—outside the camp, to bear his disgrace. This means that we are no longer identified with the camp, that is, the community of Israel on its way across the desert. We are no longer identified with the city; we are no longer inside the gate of Jerusalem, safe and snug; we are outside at the place of the skull, the gallows hill where good people do not stay very long, where they perform their grisly duty to society posthaste and then rush back where there is order and sanity, life and health and warmth.

But what does it mean to go outside the camp and to bear the reproach of Christ?

What did it mean to the Hebrews, to whom this letter is written from the brethren in Italy some time in the eighties of the first century?

It must have meant that since Christ had fulfilled the sacrifice of the old faith, Christians must now no longer depend upon the Jewish faith or the Jewish cultus for salvation. If we are to believe our date, the Temple of Jerusalem was no longer standing when this letter was written. It had fallen a decade earlier under the terrible Roman bombardment. But whatever the fate of the Temple, Jewish Christians were now to trust only Christ's perfect sacrifice for their salvation. It must mean this, but it means more. To go outside the camp and to share the reproach of Christ means not only to cease trusting the externals of the Jewish faith but to cease trusting the wonderful and bewildering civilization growing up around them: Roman power and magnificence, Roman order and know-how, the splendid, glittering, complex organism which was the empire in the closing decades of the first century. To go outside the camp was not only to leave Jerusalem behind but Rome as well. To suffer the reproach of Christ was to come to some sort of final reckoning with the world.

One fall when the leaves were turning I drove west through Illinois where the gigantic new tollways were being built. It was toward evening and the sunlight fell somberly through masses of cloud upon a world of bronze and fading gold. Against the western sky like the ribcage of some cosmic beast there rose up the piers and buttresses, the vaults and substructures of the new roads. At that distance the men working on the project looked like inconsequential ants and their immense machinery like nursery toys. I was gripped by the melancholy of history, what the Germans call *Weltschmerz*, the agony of seeing re-enacted before my eyes the glory of Rome. The toll-road could well have been an aqueduct bringing water into the Eternal City, and the workers, Roman slaves laying stone upon stone.

The first century of our era saw a frenzy of such building: roads, harbors, aqueducts, fora, baths—the Roman gentleman's athletic club—stadia, circuses, theaters, temples, and private dwellings—magnificent complexes of marble, tile, and mosaic surrounded by gardens and parks, splashing fountains and sparkling pools. Everywhere there was building, expansion, integration. The Roman road system and the waters of the Mediterranean bound the nation together with the sinews of stone and green water, and in the remotest towns and cities of the empire the local citizens toiled to make their town a mirroring of the glories of Rome.

The unifying of the empire by such a system of bones, arteries, sinews, and nerves encouraged further mobility, urbanization, and centralization. Small farmers who could no longer farm profitably sold out to wealthy absentee landlords and crowded into the large cities. Here they were fed at public expense, housed in large apartment buildings constructed by the state, and entertained at the municipal stadia and circuses. Meanwhile, more and more slaves were imported into the cities, throwing the older artisans out of work. But commerce was brisk and industry vigorous, and gold stolen from the conquered provinces still pumped life into the national economy.

Harbors were crowded, the sea was full of sails, and the roads were loud with the clomping of hooves and the tread of marching legionnaires.

It was a proud, strong, glittering time, dedicated to the pursuit of money, status, and pleasure. There has never been a time in the history of mankind when so much ingenuity and money was lavished on contrived amusement and when people worked so hard to be happy. Happiness was, in fact, a vocation and a business for many. Slaves were killed to support it, and eventually the slaughter of Christians became the *pièce de résistance*, the main feature of an afternoon performance.

Nations need more than roads and walls to bind them together, and the tragedy of Rome was that it had less and less of the coherence of faith, love, and hope. The old religions were gone or going—the butt of public ridicule and the victim of neglect. The emperor replaced the gods, but the emperor was frequently a knave, a fool, or a coward; it was difficult to feel devotional when worshiping a murderer or a pervert. The love of country also disappeared and this admirable motive was replaced by money. Where formerly a soldier had died for Rome because he wanted to defend it, he now fought for Rome at his own convenience because he was paid for it. Gradually the personnel of the legions became barbarian: men who did not know Rome or knew it only to hate it. What was true of love of country was true also of the love of family. The old Roman monogamy rotted before the onslaught of urban corruptions and vices, and even the Roman matron, once the model of virtue, could now be seen on dissolute expeditions to the hot spots of Alexandria and Rome.

With the loss of faith and love came also the loss of hope.

The Rome which had once been an expanding circle, constantly pushing back the borders of conquest, reached its natural limits, prepared its fortifications, and waited. Beyond the Roman walls fresh and vigorous barbarian hordes gathered themselves for the assault. In almost any provincial city Roman elite retired at night with a vague feeling of anxiety and unrest. There seemed almost always a barbarian face peering in at the window.

Despair was not limited to national perspectives. In the hectic activity of the Romans during the dying centuries one senses a morbid lust for life and an equally morbid fear of death. Because life was proving to be so brief and guttering, men sought for stronger stimulants and deeper sedatives, for more corrosive pleasures which would bite and prickle and burn, and for more soothing balms and unguents. Because there was so much need to prove the livingness of life—its pulp and juice—there was also a sickly need to see men suffer, bleed, convulse, and die. It was as if only the sight of the dying made life worth living. This was not the brutality of savages but of sophisticates. It points up the ultimate perversion of a civilization which has written God off.

In this age to bear the disgrace of Christ was not merely to resist the pleasures of the world but to resist its spirit, that is, antichrist. Antichrist was he who neutralized the judgment and hence the mercy of God. To be a follower of antichrist was hence to refuse criticism and to glorify what is. It was to be enslaved to the visible, to be in love with the city and to be locked in its embrace. It was to confuse the creature and the Creator, who is blessed forever.

To bear the disgrace of Christ was to see the city of this

world as passing away and to seek the city which is to come. It was to look upon the world with a shade of melancholy; it was to distinguish, like John, between Babylon and the New Jerusalem.

There is a sense, in fact, in which the Apocalypse of John gives us an excellent commentary on the text from Hebrews. We recall the woe in chapter 18:

> After this I saw another angel coming down from heaven, having great authority; and the earth was made bright with his splendor. And he called out with a mighty voice, "Fallen, fallen is Babylon the great! It has become a dwelling place of demons, a haunt of every foul spirit, a haunt of every foul and hateful bird. . . .
>
> Then I heard another voice from heaven saying, "Come out of her, my people, lest you take part in her sins, lest you share in her plagues; for her sins are heaped high as heaven, and God has remembered her iniquities. . . .
>
> And the kings of the earth, who committed fornication and were wanton with her, will weep and wail over her when they see the smoke of her burning; they will stand far off, in fear of her torment, and say, "Alas! alas! thou great city, thou mighty city, Babylon! In one hour has thy judgment come." And the merchants of the earth weep and mourn for her, since no one buys their cargo any more, cargo of gold, silver, jewels and pearls, fine linen, purple, silk and scarlet, all kinds of scented wood, all articles of ivory, all articles of costly wood, bronze, iron and marble, cinnamon, spice, incense, myrrh, frankincense, wine, oil, fine flour and wheat, cattle and sheep, horses and chariots, and slaves, that is, human souls. "The fruit for which thy soul longed has gone from thee, and all thy dainties and thy splendor are lost to thee, never to be found again!" The merchants of these

wares, who gained wealth from her, will stand far off, in fear of her torment, weeping and mourning aloud, "Alas, alas, for the great city that was clothed in fine linen, in purple and scarlet, bedecked with gold, with jewels, and with pearls! In one hour all this wealth has been laid waste." And all shipmasters and seafaring men, sailors and all whose trade is on the sea, stood far off and cried out as they saw the smoke of her burning, "What city was like the great city?" And they threw dust on their heads, as they wept and mourned, crying out, "Alas, alas, for the great city where all who had ships at sea grew rich by her wealth! In one hour she has been laid waste. Rejoice over her, O heaven, O saints and apostles and prophets, for God has given judgment for you against her!"

Then a mighty angel took up a stone like a great millstone and threw it into the sea, saying, "So shall Babylon the great city be thrown down with violence, and shall be found no more; and the sound of harpers and minstrels, of flute players and trumpeters, shall be heard in thee no more; and a craftsman of any craft shall be found in thee no more; and the sound of the millstone shall be heard in thee no more; and the light of a lamp shall shine in thee no more; and the voice of bridegroom and bride shall be heard in thee no more; for thy merchants were the great men of the earth, and all nations were deceived by thy sorcery. And in her was found the blood of prophets and of saints, and of all who have been slain on earth."

As a foil for the condemned city John gives us, like the writer of Hebrews, a city whose builder is God.

Then I saw a new heaven and a new earth; for the first heaven and the first earth had passed away, and the sea was no more. And I saw the holy city, new Jerusalem, coming down out of heaven from God, prepared as a bride adorned for her husband; and I heard a great voice from the throne saying, "Behold, the dwelling of God is with men. He will dwell with them, and they shall be his people, and God himself will be with them; he will wipe away every tear from their eyes, and death shall be no more, neither shall there be mourning nor crying nor pain any more, for the former things have passed away" (Revelation 20:1-4).

But, we ask, what does the disgrace of Christ mean to us? Its meaning for the Christian minority of the first century is certainly this rejection of antichrist and the Babylonian harlot, but what is its meaning for us? We are not a minority but a majority, at least in terms of influence, throughout the Western world. What does it mean to contemporary Protestants to go outside the camp and bear the reproach of Christ?

Actually the meaning has not changed too much. To be identified with the dying Christ is still to be identified with the heavenly victory, the invisible triumph. It is to be a pilgrim seeking another city. It is to lack some of that massive security which develops in a spirit entirely at home in the world: the solidity of power, of technique, of influence. To be a Christian in today's world and to be Christ's exile and wanderer is to be somewhat transparent, to have an identity not quite my own, to be curiously double. I live, yet not I. Or in the words of John, "He must increase and I must decrease."

This means that for me to be visibly successful is not the most important thing of all. In our world *not* to be visibly successful is to be nothing; to be visibly successful is to be everything. I need not succeed in terms of wealth or power or even wisdom. It is possible to succeed visibly as a saint. It is possible to succeed visibly even as a failure. What is a beatnik but an obviously successful failure?

To bear the disgrace of Christ is to hear an entirely different drummer. It is to be interested in a different set of goods. I drove not long ago along West Madison Street in Chicago. I drove slowly and I observed carefully. An old derelict drifted across the street. He was almost too good to be true. Even West Madison Street is becoming aware of itself as a film location, and it is possible that what one takes for a vagrant is an actor on his way to work. This old man was dirty, bearded, ragged, befogged. He had stuck his feet in an old pair of brogans without laces and he shuffled along unconscious of the melancholy appearance he made.

I said to myself, "No one cares whether this man lives or dies. There is no one who says, 'Joe, it's time to get up. Joe, take your bath and shave while I'm getting breakfast. Joe, I noticed that your shoes need new laces; here's a pair. Why don't you put them in? Good-by, Joe, have a good day.' Nobody said these things. Nobody was trying to make Joe a respectable anything. He was outside the pale. Outside the camp. He didn't belong any more. There was only one little world he knew. The world inside the bottle, and for this world he steered as fast as his flapping shoes would carry him." These were the things I thought on West Madison.

I am not drawing any simple parallels between a Christian bearing the disgrace of Christ and this unfortunate man. But there is a sense in which to be outside the camp means, as for this man, that some things cease to matter. Or at least they do not matter quite so much. The things inside the vanishing city are not so important as the world which is coming into existence. It is said of John Wesley—and we seem to be returning to him—that when he was once enjoined on a garden walk to admire the burning beauty of flowers and lawns, he said quite simply, "It is all very fine, but I know another world." And the other world was already within him.

Or we recall the story of St. Bernard of Clairvaux who, when he was on his way around a lake in the vicinity of his monastery, was asked by his servant if he did not think the lake water beautiful in the spring sunlight. And the great saint turned to his page and said with utter simplicity, "Lake, what lake?"

Perhaps a modern example will do. I know a very great man and an able writer who at the age of thirty was a social darling. He owned a beautiful old estate not far from Stockholm, he was married to the daughter of an enormously wealthy banker, he had a brilliant circle of friends. At his estate there were festal weekends. Good food, choice liquors, witty conversation, handsome young princes of business in elegant clothes, lovely and sophisticated women. All was light, airy, *bon vivant*. It was 1913, and everything was good in the best of all possible worlds.

One summer evening when the gardens around the old mansion were filled with people all being courteous, vivacious, and perhaps just a little naughty, my friend slipped away from the laughter and the repartee and the clink of glasses and walked down the drive which wound through stately old chestnuts to the main road. As soon as he had left the crowd behind, a great silence came over him. It was an outside silence with the midsummer sun just over the dark green forest rim and only the dying twitter of a few drowsy birds. And it was an inside quiet. The jarring impact of hours of shallow chatter faded away within him and he heard nothing except the beating of his own heart. He walked to the main gate and stood looking down the road which curved off in both directions. He stood absolutely quiet. And a voice within him said, "You must go away from this. You must leave all of it behind you."

The Christian faith when it has been truly vigorous has always had this kind of structured tentativeness. It never quite settles down. This does not mean that it yields to a sickly otherworldliness which feels no responsibility for the world. On the contrary, it is precisely its detachment, its ultimate indifference about an earthly destiny, which makes its people concerned about existence. It was the poverty of Francis which enriched his time. It is the self-denial of Christian missionaries which has made life richer for millions of people.

Paul says it so as to bring a catch to our throat:

> I mean, brethren, the appointed time has grown very short; from now on, let those who have wives live as though they had none, and those who mourn as though they were not mourning, and those who rejoice as though they were not rejoicing, and those who buy as though they had no goods, and those who deal with the world as though they had no dealings with it. For the form of this world is passing away (1 Corinthians 7:29-31).

It is people for whom the navel cord of this world has been cut who can give themselves most joyously to its redemption. That is why for the writer to the Hebrews the disgrace of Christ is not only saying farewell to the vanishing world and seeking that city which is to come. It is also offering up sacrifices of thanks to God for the reality of existence in him. Above everything else, it is doing good and sharing, that is, being agents of his benevolence. It is the same writer who encourages us to leave the city behind and to come outside the camp who also writes:

> Let brotherly love continue. Do not neglect to show hospitality to strangers, for thereby some have entertained angels unawares. Remember those who are in prison, as though in prison with them; and those who are ill-treated, since you also are in the body. (Hebrews 13:1-3)

VII. *"If we confess . . . ."*

That which was from the beginning, which we have heard, which we have seen with our eyes, which we have looked upon and touched with our hands, concerning the word of life—the life was made manifest, and we saw it, and testify to it, and proclaim to you the eternal life which was with the Father and was made manifest to us—that which we have seen and heard we proclaim also to you, so that you may have fellowship with us; and our fellowship is with the Father and with his Son Jesus Christ. And we are writing this that our joy may be complete.

This is the message we have heard from him and proclaim to you, that God is light and in him is no darkness at all. If we say we have fellowship with him while we walk in darkness, we lie and do not live according to the truth; but if we walk in the light, as he is in the light, we have fellowship with one another, and the blood of Jesus his Son cleanses us from all sin. If we say we have no sin, we deceive ourselves, and the truth is not in us. If we confess our sins, he is faithful and just, and will forgive our sins and cleanse us from all unrighteousness. If we say we have not sinned, we make him a liar, and his word is not in us.

I JOHN 1:1-10

A ROMAN PRIEST I once knew was unhappy about the word *fellowship*. He was jovial enough, but to his cool, liturgical mind fellowship had a chummy smell; he associated it with phoniness and sentimentality. For him the church is massive and austere—a citadel with bastions, within which men and women are saved from damnation. The body of Christ is so vast in time and place and so diamond-hard in substance that to confuse it with the soft clottings of fellowship is scandalous. In its dogma and worship, the strength of its hierarchy, and the ponderousness of its law the church ignores the impulses of individuals, smiles indulgently at the minor rebellions of sects and cults, and even disposes of major revolutions by a shrug of the shoulders. Fellowship—bah!

We may have other reasons than the Roman Catholics for distrusting the word *fellowship*. Our age is full of such terms as *togetherness*, *teamwork*, and even *groupiness*. Isolated and unhappy people having lost the older structures of family, tribe, and community tend more and more to squash together in miscellaneous and brief unities. Such flimsy grounds for oneness as height, color of hair, disposition, age, and even tenancy of a suburban block press people together like bruised fruit. Out of real need for society comes such a bizarre invention as the block party with its broiled steaks and pathetic brittleness. It is closeness of a sort and fellowship of a sort: the conversation flows easily about outboard horsepower and the price of bourbon and the increase in millage for the new school, and the new blonde, but it has mush at the heart.

Fellowship nevertheless remains man's best hope. A community of truth and love in which tensions and hostilities are overcome and in which men work together for the achievement of a common blessedness—this is the essence of utopian dreams which have instructed and sometimes inspired mankind. Philosophers, social statesmen, poets, and lately psychologists and sociologists have grubbed for the causes of group apathy and group hatred, always with the hope that the application of a remedy, the removal of some accidental malignity, would bring about soundness in the communal body and assure fellowship. Family relations, labor relations, international relations, race relations—all these speak of our wish that with the application of greater discernment and the bleaching of our emotions, the true *koinonia* may emerge.

It was the hope of the world in which John wrote his epistles. In the eastern empire the infant gospel met a variety of cults which believed that man could attain fellowship with the divine through mystical and secret disciplines. The knowledge of God was an ascent by tortuous ladders, and fellowship with God was the apex of illumination: the eighty-sixth merit badge of a graying Eagle Scout.

Against this false view of salvation John levels the truth of the primitive gospel: the eternal life which was with the Father was made manifest to us . . . and our fellowship is with the Father and with his Son, Jesus Christ.

There is no way of seeing or embracing God except through Christ. There is no fellowship with the Father that is not first of all fellowship with the Son. And there is no fellowship with the Father and Son except through the mystery of the passion.

The way to fellowship with God is hence through an acceptance of the truth of the incarnation and of the passion. "Jesus Christ has come in the flesh," and "he is the expiation for our sins." This is the essential message. To claim fellowship with God without embracing the truth of Christ is to walk in darkness; it is to lie and not to live according to the truth.

But what, you ask, does all this mean? What does it mean to me? What are salvation, incarnation, light, darkness, fellowship to me struggling with viruses and taxes, and hoodlums and hepatitis, and my own private neurosis? To this we can only answer: Much in every way. To walk in the light as he is in the light, that is, to embrace the truth of Christ, is to see with wide-eyed wonder and with great humility both what God is and what I am. It is in Wilder's phrase, to let "our lives be ordered by reality, by things as they are."[14]

The reality of the gospel, that is, of the incarnation, is nevertheless not so easily accessible as we might think. We do not move up to the microscope, observe, and make a notation. The revelation of God is not smoothly plausible like those religious systems which jostled one another in the great cities of Asia Minor and Africa. It is in many ways a harsh and crooked story, marked by riddle and paradox. It asks us to believe that God permitted himself to be born as a naked and wailing infant; to walk the roads of a minor Roman province as an itinerant preacher called Jesus of Nazareth; to fall into the hands of a gang of politicians and be murdered as a disturber of the peace. It asks us to accept as true that this indignity had as its aim to reconcile men to God. And finally it proclaims as the capstone of the whole audacious structure that Jesus was raised from the dead and became the first fruits of those who had fallen asleep. That is, that in and through the raising of Jesus, men may have eternal life and an entirely new species of fellowship.

To walk in the light is to let this message grip me: it is to let the truth of the gospel lay hold of me. It is to give attention to the terrible drama of Jesus as God's act to restore men to fellowship with him. It is to see the mysterious and urgent compassion of a God who did not spare his own son but offered him up for us all.

But to walk in the light is more than this. It is to see and to accept as a most bitter fact that the cause of the murder of Abel and the murder of Christ and hence of the fracture of all relationships lies in the mystery of human iniquity and of my iniquity. That the death of the family and the death of the community and the death of civilization root themselves in a perversity as dear to me as my own flesh.

To walk in the light is to look with the cold objectivity of Augustine upon his boyhood in Tagaste. The incident of the pear theft which is brushed aside by the morally liberated as a childish lunge in the direction of maturity is seen by Augustine from the perspective of man's involvement in rebellion and in shame. He writes:

> But I, I wanted to steal, and I did it compelled by no want. . . . For I stole what I already possessed in abundance and of much better quality. Nor did I desire to enjoy the thing itself which was the object of my inclination to steal, but the very act of stealing, the sin itself.
>
> There was a pear tree near our vineyard which was laden with fruit that was attractive neither in appearance nor in taste. In the dead of night—for we had prolonged our playing in the vacant lots according to our usual unhealthy custom, until then—we crept up to it, a gang of youthful

> good-for-nothings, to shake it down and despoil it. We carried away huge loads, not as a treat for ourselves, but just to throw to the pigs. Of course, we did eat a few, but we did so only to be doing something which would be pleasant because forbidden.
>
> Look at my heart, O God, look at my heart, which thou hast pitied in the depth of the abyss; look at my heart; may it tell Thee now what I saw in this. . . . It was filthy and I loved it. I loved my own destruction. I loved my own fault; not the object to which I directed my faulty action, but my fault itself, was what I loved, my vile soul leaping down from Thy support into extinction, not shamefully coveting anything, but coveting shame itself.[15]

To walk in the light is to see mankind thus: to find in all the switchblades and bicycle chains and brutal beatings and meaningless destruction the malice of Dante's Hell. And it is to see myself thus: a city with vacant lots overrun by hoodlums, crossed and recrossed by vagrant impulses, echoing with laughter.

Let us make due allowance for all those sicknesses which the newer psychology has found to cling like barnacles to the human spirit. Let us accept, at least as a working hypothesis, the presence of urges, frustrations, suppressed hostilities, fears, lusts, and perversions which cover the ground of infancy like fleshy and obscene toadstools. And let us by all means institute those programs of mental health which will cleanse our minds and restore them to soundness. Let us be careful about the toilet training of our children, the role of authority, the Oedipal constructions and reconstructions, and the warmth of our parental feelings. Let us pursue relentlessly those morbid symptoms which mask perversions under the guise of religion. Let us look at Augustine's relations to his mother and St. Francis' problem with his father image.

But let us not imagine that when we have restored the emotions to reasonable health we have done anything ultimate with the spirit. It was not a sadistic impulse that brought Jesus to the cross, but something more deeply human. It was man's urge to be God that impelled him to do God in. To walk in the light is to focus upon this bitter fact and to see it as the poisonous ingredient in all of existence. If we say we have no sin, we deceive ourselves and the truth is not in us.

Contemporary life is filled with the efforts of men to circumvent this dark truth. The revolt against the Puritans which began a hundred years ago and which speaks in the language of Pater and Swinburne and Whitman and Lawrence and Wallace Stevens is an endeavor to dissolve the guilt-ridden negatives of the Christian past in the hot sunlight of affirmation. Stevens' "Sunday Morning" is a poem about a woman who feels this active hostility toward the *good* past:

> Shall she not find in comforts of the sun
> In pungent fruit and bright green wings, or else
> In any balm or beauty of the earth,
> Things to be cherished like the thought of heaven?[16]

She will at least seek. She will seek by enlightenment and suntan lotion and long days on southern beaches and bright winters in utterly linear rooms with clear glass and glossy panels and the dull sheen of smooth expensive metals: in everything that is shadow-proof and uninvolved to free herself of the somber crookedness of guilt. But she will not find.

The refusal to face the open riddle of our iniquity plunges

us into a whole range of deceptions. We beguile ourselves into believing that we are better than we are. We fool ourselves into believing that we ourselves and our families and our clan, our class, our race, and our club, and even our country are good in a special way and stand outside the need of redemption.

It is the merit of much modern literature that it sees some of the problem. In a pitiless way it strips away the veil from our most intimate and tender relationships. It finds the will to power in the caresses of a mother and murderous rage behind the filial piety of obedient children. It questions a whole range of virtues: the fidelities of married life, the heroism of patriots, the self-effacement of priests. In the fellowship of all human unities it finds exploitation, traffic, and fury. It is well that it should be so that no flesh, not even Christian flesh, should glory in His presence.

But even the secular prophets whose strictures against the middle class are so cleanly venomous are not without sin. The black sweaters, the naked stove-pipe and slop-bucket and milk drunk from a carton and dog-eared paperbacks and collectively contemplated navels and mystical identification with the outcasts of Guadalupe Hidalgo—these things are not rungs on the ladder of salvation. Even among the holy-unholy, angry, and bitter men the ape and the tiger, the snake and goat, gibber and growl and slither and bray.

To walk in the light is to confess this. Not to state or to grovel meanly but to confess. To acknowledge that I am this sort of man, in part because this is what I choose to be. And to acknowledge it with sorrow. And to turn when I confess not merely toward the altar or toward the anonymous neck in the pew ahead of me but to turn with gravity toward the other, the brother. To look into his eyes and to see the pain within the pupil, the sickness and the burden not only of our shared mortality but our shared transgression. To confess is to walk in the light.

And to confess is to accept the only availing remedy: the blood of Jesus his Son.

> For whatever is born of God overcomes the world; and this is the victory that overcomes the world, our faith. Who is it that overcomes the world but he who believes that Jesus is the Son of God? This is he who came by water and blood, Jesus Christ, not with the water only but with the water and the blood. And the Spirit is the witness, because the Spirit is the truth. There are three witnesses, the Spirit, the water, and the blood; and these three agree (1 John 5:4-8).

Again we face the riddle of the incarnation. To accept God's coming in the flesh is to accept the gift of expiation and reconciliation, that is, the scandal of his blood. The blood of Christ is the death of God. Like the sacrifice of Isaac it is the giving up of the identity and the blessing and all the time to come. For what is left to the Father once the Son is dead? And the death of Christ is the sacrifice of the firstborn that he might be the birth pang of many brethren. And the blood of Christ is the life of God coursing through the body of Christ which is his church, cleansing, reconciling, healing. The blood of Christ is the only remedy for the mangled limbs of community.

There are difficulties with the dogma of the blood. The how. How is the blood of Christ made efficacious? There gathers around this truth the endless debate of the theologians. In France in the tenth century rats nibbled some consecrated wafers, and Scotus Erigena was asked for an opinion of the effect of the act on their rodent natures. In Germany in the sixteenth century a Lutheran woman spilled some of the consecrated wine from a chalice on her fur coat. She was enjoined to burn it. In the seventeenth century Calvinists called Lutherans cannibals because of their doctrine of communion. In the eighteenth century the great Zinzendorf and his followers developed a wildly exaggerated mysticism and spoke of themselves as "blood worms." But no formulation of the mystery within classical Christianity has affected the central faith of the church that it is Christ's atoning death on the cross which makes the difference between truth and falsehood, light and darkness, life and death. If we confess our sins, he is faithful and just, and will forgive our sins and cleanse us from all unrighteousness.

He is faithful and just.

There are difficulties with the dogma. There is no difficulty with the fact. The life of the church is the dynamic confrontation of sin and forgiveness. The body of the church—this ponderous, aged colossus—lives one breath away from death. It is kept alive—if it lives at all—through the unending rhythm of confession and new mercy. It will not do to seek for it an Olympian immortality. Both we and the church stand not only in the need of prayer but of oxygen. During the centuries all sorts of theological solutions have been proposed which would circumvent the need of a daily humiliation. One lay Christian tried to assure me that salvation was a one-shot inoculation, as if grace were some sort of horse serum. But grace is not vaccination; it is breathing and finding my lungs filled with air. Modern sculpture which rejects the egglike smoothness of marbled surfaces tries to say this. The human figure should be rough and pocked, the eyes should be red-rimmed and aching from seeking the vision of God.

The church and its people live in this unending rhythm of confession and mercy. This is the meaning of communion. We come like starving men to receive the bread of grace.

In confession lies also the hope of fellowship: not of phoniness or groupiness but of fellowship: a relationship of truth and love in which I dare confess my sin to my brother and he dares to forgive me for Christ's sake.

In such a *koinonia* there begins to flicker that flame of joy which points beyond itself to completeness.

VIII. *The Passion and the* Kosmos

And when they have finished their testimony, the beast that ascends from the bottomless pit will make war upon them and conquer them and kill them, and their dead bodies will lie in the street of the great city which is allegorically called Sodom and Egypt, where their Lord was crucified. For three days and a half men from the peoples and tribes and tongues and nations gaze at their dead bodies and refuse to let them be placed in a tomb, and those who dwell on the earth will rejoice over them and make merry and exchange presents, because these two prophets had been a torment to those who dwell on the earth. But after the three and a half days a breath of life from God entered them, and they stood up on their feet, and great fear fell on those who saw them. REVELATION 11:7-11

PERHAPS we are getting used to corpses. Singly in detective fiction they provide the joys of a socially accepted sadism (the body at the foot of the stairs); massed they form the somber backdrop of our time (bobbing torsos at Iwo, "meat wagons" bringing back the fallen from the lines, at Dachau piles of clayey pallor and the humility of humbled flesh: the deferential skull, the flaccid breasts, the belly cavernous between the hip blades, the genitals unobtrusive, the fleshless buttocks bared in shame).

But whether or not this is so, the two bodies in the Apocalypse shake us. They swim into focus in a glut of bizarre images which seem contemporary in their distortions. There are falling stars and flaming mountains and blooded seas; there are men and beasts pasted together in a surrealistic montage (locusts with iron wings and human faces and the hair of women and crowns of gold). But the two bodies in the street give us the authentic shudder.

The bodies are the mundane center of the Apocalypse. They are martyrs who have been killed because of their witness. In the telescopic manner characteristic of the book, they probably represent both Moses and Elijah (law and prophet) and Peter and Paul (witnesses to Jew and Gentile).[17] The Apocalypse is in some sense the song of Moses and the Lamb; the slain martyrs represent the whole tradition of Judaeo-Christian witness as well as its mournful destiny in the world of men and demons.

The book has the concreteness and the universality of a morality play. The bodies in the street are more than the flesh of heroic men. They are the arena of a cosmic struggle. Around these desecrated remains the energies of God and Satan are polarized. God sends the witnesses to speak his truth; they are overcome and slain by a demonic beast from the bottomless pit. For a mystical interval—three and a half days—there is a momentary retreat of the divine presence, and the bodies become the focus of a feast of joyous abandonment. The festival has the character of a black Christmas: the victors, men and women, sway drunkenly in a dance of triumph, clutch and squeeze one another with uproarious laughter, and send off gifts. The children are present too, their gargoyle faces raised in impudence. They dart here and there, spitting on the corpses and landing furtive kicks on their posteriors.

It is, of course, a religious feast. The martyrs are those who will not deify the emperor, will not drop a pinch of incense before the image, will not compose the features in awe. The martyrs are those who will not call man God. They will do everything else which the state requires. They will honor the emperor as the divinely appointed head of the government; they will even pray for him. They will pray for Claudius, Nero, Domitian. They will pay taxes and live in quiet obedience to the laws of the empire. But they will not idolize. This is their crime. They are not good Romans. When they die, the patriots rejoice.

The scene of the desecration shares in the particular universality of the victims. We are told that the city is the great city where their Lord also was crucified. This would make it Jerusalem, but the mystical designations "Sodom" and "Egypt" suggest a wider meaning. The martyrs die at the nexus of divine purpose and human rebellion, whatever its cultural particularity. The "great city" is the brickyards on the green Egyptian delta where the Israelites toiled and grumbled, the precincts of Sodom where the family of Lot lived in holy isolation, the imperial gardens of Rome where living torches lighted up the dark. It is the palace of Ahab and Herod.

The vision of John telescopes sacred history and geography; it is the confluence of all events and places and powers. Around the two unburied bodies the protagonists of good and evil arrange themselves. In a sense the issue has already been decided; the key to it may be glimpsed in the heavenlies. The throne is there and the seals and the angels and the trumpets. The Lamb is there also, and his death is the heart of the triumph. But the heavenly victory is not yet particularized, and there is arrayed against the witnesses a host of grisly beings: beasts and dragons and demons.

The mood of the Apocalypse is not our mood. In spite of our penetration into space, or perhaps because of it, we have no interest in relating the individual to the cosmic. The *kosmos* has no inner meaning for us. The destiny of people and of communities is not interwoven any longer with the mysterious unfoldment of the universe. In John's day everything was populated and hence personalized. Even for the heretics the ascent into the dizzying heavenlies was not conceived of as a trip but as a pilgrimage. It involved will and feeling and intellect. In our day people take trips. Some sort of conveyance picks them up and transports them physically from here to there. The airlines and shipping lines and travel agencies vie with one another to remove the element of choice from the journey. They are concerned about washing out the frictive: to make the trip so predictable that one simple decision will suffice. To go or not to go.

And what is space travel but an extension in terms of distance and complexity of the Cook's Tour? Here too, the purpose is to remove the risk, the friction, the volition.

One of the Russian spacemen has been ridiculed because he claims not to have seen any sign of God at two hundred miles distance from the earth. But he has a point. We do not sense a universe of will poised against us or for us unless our motion through space is a pilgrimage, that is, unless we accept our destiny as men and are willing to use our arms and our legs.

The loss of a cosmic framework has given our arena a curiously limited scope. The battlefield is now confined to the diameter of a man's skull. In London in 1962 I saw Osborne's *Luther*. I am not sure I understood the play, but I saw and heard enough to be impressed by the suffocating "narrowness" of the thesis. I use "narrowness" advisedly. The play was imaginative and, in its way, powerful. But Luther's crisis turned out to be a relieved colon, and the Reformation hinged on a bowel movement. Osborne is not the first to use these humble acts as a literary vehicle, but in Rabelais and Swift the scatological is universal and comical; it has dimension. In Osborne I sensed only an essential distrust of time and space.

The depopulation of space is a greater catastrophe than we imagine. It gives us the Bermuda of the travel circulars instead of the one in Shakespeare's *Tempest*. He was never physically in contact with that enchantingly windswept, blue-green world, but if you have been in Bermuda, you know that he *knew* it, that he rooted it out with the frantic motion of his senses. Its essence was in his nostrils and on his tongue.

It is in this sense that John, inspired by a greater spirit, knew the world. He smelled the rank upon rank of powers gathered with the clanking of arms and the smell of horse dung and the shouts of the soldiery. For him the air was crammed with meaning. He saw it as an enormous wheel with the spokes converging on a hub. Cosmogony has nothing to do with it. We are not talking about the size of the universe or even its many centers of interest. We are talking about the world as one center of interest and in that world a burning focus of attention: the martyr witness. What happened to these two men in the city where their Lord was crucified really mattered not only to them but to the *kosmos*. For a few moments heaven was silent and so, we may be sure, was hell.

The ability to see the world this way is most rare in our day. Even Christians think largely of "personality adjustment" or "emotional health," which means that I am alone in the midst of my cauliflower brain and the few pallid chestnuts which are my glands. C. S. Lewis, Dorothy Sayers, T. S. Eliot, Charles Williams, and a few others have tried to explode this cranial universe and catapult us into the larger world where we encounter not only flesh and blood but principalities and powers. But most of us doubt it or fear it. If we are going "out" or "up," we prefer a sophisticated milk can on the business end of a missile.

A fine protest against this aseptically sterile universe is Lewis' science fiction, particularly *That Hideous Strength*.[18] The latter is a sort of morality play in novel form. The foci of interest are N.I.C.E. (the National Institute of Co-ordinated Experiments), a nasty collection of dehumanized scientists who intend to make over mankind; and St. Anne's, a Christian hospice and a beachhead of the angelic world. Lewis calls the book a "tall story about devilry," and it is "tall" indeed. But it comes close to the spirit of the Apocalypse. The fates of Mark Studdock and his wife Jane matter to the powers of darkness and to those of light. They are pawns to be reckoned with on the great cosmic chessboard. It is thus with the two dead witnesses in our text. They matter. They matter to hell, and they matter to heaven. Not only are they the center of a circle with a gigantic radius; their death is the first link of a chain of events, the beginning of a drama which moves rapidly toward the denouement.

Behind and above this momentous episode is the primal event itself: *the passion of Christ.* The meaning of the two witnesses must be read in the protomartyrdom of Christ: "where also their Lord was crucified." Much sense and nonsense have been written about John's vision, and all sorts of parallels have been drawn with Persian, Zoroastrian, and Judaic models. We need not quarrel with the scholars whose lifework it is to find "parallels" and "influences." May peace attend them! But what is obvious even to a child who may not find his way through "allusions" and "apocalyptic symbolism" is that the celestial center of the book—the secret of the cryptogram—is "Jesus Christ and him crucified." He it is who is worthy to open the seal of the scroll of judgment and to receive the adoration of the celestial world.

> Then I looked, and I heard around the throne and the living creatures and the elders the voice of many angels, numbering

> myriads of myriads and thousands of thousands, saying with a loud voice, "Worthy is the Lamb who was slain, to receive power and wealth and wisdom and might and honor and glory and blessing!" And I heard every creature in heaven and on earth and under the earth and in the sea, and all therein, saying, "To him who sits upon the throne and to the Lamb be blessing and honor and glory and might for ever and ever!" (Revelation 5:11-13)

The triumph of Christ thus becomes the guarantee of the victory of the desecrated bodies in the street of the great city. Christ has conquered; his death has triggered the awe-inspiring motion of the chariots of judgment. Soon now—very soon—after a mystical interlude of three and a half days, the wheels will move. The witnesses will be restored to life and assumed to heaven. And the souls of those who have been "slain for the word of God and for the witness they have borne" will be consoled.

> When he opened the fifth seal, I saw under the altar the souls of those who had been slain for the word of God and for the witness they had borne; they cried out with a loud voice, "O Sovereign Lord, holy and true, how long before thou wilt judge and avenge our blood on those who dwell upon the earth?" Then they were each given a white robe and told to rest a little longer, until the number of their fellow servants and their brethren should be complete, who were to be killed as they themselves had been. (Revelation 6:9-11)

The essence of the consolation is that in a little while the mystical number of those destined to be slain for their testimony will be complete. The meaning of this is not shallowly fatalistic. John is not giving a celestial timetable so much as an assurance that the death of the martyrs has its place in the unfoldment of the divine purpose. Everything matters: the death of Christ, the death of the souls under the altar, the death of the two witnesses, and the death of those who now live under the terrible shadow of persecution.

It is in this context we must read the anxious question of the saints under the altar, "How long before thou wilt judge and avenge our blood on those who dwell upon the earth?" The question can be charged with vindictiveness, as indeed it is by at least one scholar. Martin Rist writes, "This hope of persecuted Christians that God will avenge them is at least understandable, even though it may be regarded as far from commendable. . . . This attitude . . . is quite different from that attributed to Jesus on the cross . . . or to Stephen."[19] But Rist is chargeable with two common fallacies. The first is to assume that the word of Jesus or Stephen neutralizes what each said in other contexts about judgment. If we eliminate from the words of Jesus all that he said in indignation or warning of coming judgment, we have a badly gutted gospel. And the words of Stephen which purportedly led to his stoning were certainly not in the spirit of a "gentle Jesus, meek and mild."

The second fallacy is to assume that the desire for historic fulfillment is per se sub-Christian. If we believe in the reality of evil, are we not anxious to see it vanquished and the good victorious? And is not the liquidation of evil always unpleasant? Does anyone who has lived through the horror of the concentration camps imagine that such an evil can be disposed of without the treading of the winepress of God's wrath? Would an inmate of one of these hells be less a Christian if he asked when in God's name this obscenity would cease; if he wondered how long his case would have to wait before coming to trial? Or is it assumed that a Christian can never be a plaintiff, even before the bar of ultimate justice?

The crucial point here is nevertheless not what the dead under the altar are saying so much as the assurance to living Christians that the time of suffering will be short and that in the final reckoning Christ will triumph.

We turn now from the scenes on earth and in heaven to these primitive Christians.

The Apocalypse is, as we have already suggested, a letter to concrete people. It is addressed to men and women confronting particular situations; it is not intended to be, what it has sometimes become, a parlor puzzle in eschatology. The test of its relevance is historic and existential need. In periods of oppression, persecution, and imminent disaster the book has recovered some of its primitive freshness, and this ought to be a clue to how it should be read. It has been a book for proletarians, sectaries, prisoners, semiheretics, and pneumatics: people under somebody's heel or people troubled by the impossibility of staying alive another minute.

The criticism has been leveled against it by well-tailored theological professors in reasonably sheltered circumstances that it lacks Christian content. It has been said that the gospel of grace is thinly represented and that the teaching of the church on matters such as the love of one's neighbor is almost entirely lacking. This may well be, but if the Apocalypse is a tract on how to stay alive in a shipwreck or in atomic fallout, we should probably excuse the writer from developing a leisurely treatise. The book has a single purpose: to keep the church loyal to its Lord. It understands temptation as a threat to this simple but splendid quality.

The letters to the seven churches warn against the loss of fervor, the distraction of heresy (mysterious aberrations like the Nicolaitans and the synagogue of Satan), and the licentiousness of the pagans (Revelation 2 and 3). They encourage burning devotion to the faith by holding out the rewards of endurance. This is not a richly calibrated theology, for reasons already stated; against the background of Pauline and Johannine thought it has a curiously austere and even bitter quality. The faces which emerge from the pages are spare and the eyes burn. But, like the Letter to the Hebrews, it is designed for people about to be thrown to the lions. In these circumstances the need is not so much ethical as religious. It is crucial to confess and not to betray; it is crucial to be oneself a sacrifice rather than to sacrifice to an obscene divinity. It is crucial to resist.

A pathetic little story I once read about a Huguenot girl makes the mood of the Apocalypse more understandable.[20] It has a legendary quality like Foxe's *Book of Martyrs*, but this does not spoil its effect. In the late seventeenth century in the town of Aigues-Mortes in southern France, a girl named Marie Durant was brought before the authorities, charged with the Huguenot heresy. She was fourteen years old, bright, attractive, marriageable. She was asked to abjure the Huguenot faith. She was not asked to commit an immoral act, to become a criminal, or even to change the day-to-day quality of her behavior. She was only asked to say, "*J'abjure*." No more, no less. She did not comply. Together with thirty other Huguenot women she was put into a tower by the sea.

It is not much to say *J'abjure*. It slides rather readily over the lips. It seems a small price to pay for the sweetness of youth and the dignity of marriage, for a house full of children and a place by the village well and the respect and love of neighbors. But the girl said no. For thirty-eight years she continued to say it. She would not renounce her faith. And instead of the hated word *J'abjure* she, together with her fellow martyrs, scratched on the wall of the prison tower the single word *Résistez,* resist!

The word is still seen and gaped at by tourists on the stone wall at Aigues-Mortes, but for us of another day it is as inexplicable as the mood of the Apocalypse. We do not understand the terrifying simplicity of a religious commitment which asks nothing of time and gets nothing from time. We can understand a religion which enhances time by altering the attitudes and behavior of people. But we cannot understand a faith which is not nourished by the temporal hope that tomorrow things will be better. To sit in a prison room with thirty others and to see the day change into night and summer into autumn, to feel the slow systemic changes within one's flesh: the drying and wrinkling of the skin, the loss of muscle tone, the stiffening of the joints, the slow stupefaction of the senses—to feel all this and still to persevere seems almost idiotic to a generation which has no capacity to wait and to endure.

This is nevertheless the mood of the Apocalypse. The sustenance of the martyrs is not in the cessation of police pressure. Their faith is nourished by what lies beyond history, and it is the intent of the Apocalypse not only to concretize this transhistorical world—to show them the New Jerusalem—but to show them how the passion of Christ is crucial to its existence and how their own immolation gathers meaning as a re-enactment of the death of their Lord.

Thus although the New Jerusalem is a creation of God, it is a creation in which both form and matter are the "sufferings of the present world." The passion of Christ has made possible the creation of a new order. The city is the bride of the Lamb, and the foundation of the city is formed by the twelve apostles of the Lamb. Together with God the Lamb forms the temple of the city—that is, the only needful locus of worship—as well as its light. The city's inhabitants are those written in the Lamb's book of life, and the life of the city is the river which flows from the throne of God and of the Lamb.

The relationship of the prospective martyr to the New Jerusalem need hardly be stressed. Although he does not create the city by his death—God forbid!—he is predisposed to appropriate it and in some sense to comprehend it because he is in the company of the slain. In the millennial reign of Christ the Apocalypse assigns a special place to the martyr:

> Also I saw the souls of those who had been beheaded for their testimony to Jesus and for the word of God, and who had not worshiped the beast or its image and had not received its mark on their foreheads or their hands. They came to life again, and reigned with Christ a thousand years. The rest of the dead did not come to life again until the thousand years were ended. This is the first resurrection. Blessed and holy is he who shares in the first resurrection! Over such the second death has no power, but they shall be priests of God and of Christ, and they shall reign with him a thousand years (Revelation 20:4-6).

The comfort of the Apocalypse is thus nakedly eschatological. In the midst of a situation of utmost gravity, it calls upon men and women to be faithful to the *end*. Only this. And it warns the *traditores*, the betrayers of Christ, of the melancholy culmination toward which they move.

> But as for the cowardly, the faithless, the polluted, as for murderers, fornicators, sorcerers, idolaters, and all liars, their lot shall be in the lake that burns with fire and brimstone, which is the second death (Revelation 21:8).

In spite of its great literary power, the book strikes us as unbelievably crude. Sophisticated as we are and suspicious of blacks and whites, we would like a little more nuance. The Apocalypse gives us none. For John there are two kinds of people: the faithful and the faithless, the sealed and the unsealed.

But the obvious crudity ought not blind us to the immense significance of what is said. Christianity is a hot faith. It sees existence as divided between the worship of God and the worship of idols. To be a Christian is to look with naïve directness at all the seductions of history. It is to see Rome not only as the charming hostess of an elegant estate but as the dread harlot arrayed in scarlet, and bedecked with gold and jewels and pearls, drunk with the blood of the saints and the blood of the martyrs of Jesus.

To be a Christian is to look at unrighteousness not only as inadvisable but as loathsome. We talk much about substituting a rational for a prerational and *tabu* morality. We delight in endless reservations, exceptions, modifications, and refinements. We search diligently for reasons why men and particularly we men behave as we do. And we lose our moral passion. Sin is no longer exceedingly sinful. We fear nothing and are revolted by nothing in the whole dreary catalogue of depravity.

The Apocalypse brings us back to an honest and saving crudity. It breaks the enchantment of the Bower of Bliss and lets us see the demonic lineaments in the face of the lovely lady.

It helps us feel that there are some things which are always morally repugnant and should be so considered. There are acts of "heart-whoredom"—to quote the Puritan divines—which are like caresses rendered up to the great harlot. To be a coward, whatever the justification, to be a traitor, whatever the excuse, to mire myself down in corruption, to murder by weapon or by cold malice, to yield sillily to contemporary sex worship, to connive with the Lord of Cunning and to adore him—this is to betray Christ and to give him over again into the hands of lawless men.

Living as we do in the age of cataclysmic hatreds and unholy loves as well as of monumental indifference, when we cannot bestir ourselves either to hate or love, we ought to get one simple matter straight. To be a Christian today is to be a fellow of Christ's passion. It is to be a *confessor* in the ancient sense, that is, a man who takes his position regardless of the consequences. It is to be hot. In this ongoing night in which again and again he is betrayed, it is not to betray. To be now and then frightened and confused and doubting and stupid and selfish—to be all these perhaps—but not to relinquish the first love, not to cool, not to betray. This is what the Apocalypse wants to tell us.

We have come to the end of our brief pilgrimage to the cross. We have stood together with Paul and Peter, John and Luke and the author of Hebrews, and we know not how many other first-century Christians in the circle of Christ's passion. We realize what it meant for them. Salvation and forgiveness and new life, cleansing, regeneration, sanctity, and perhaps martyrdom. Is it presumptuous to ask what the passion means to us and to ask as well if we are willing to go to him outside the camp and to share his disgrace? For it is most certainly true that only those who are willing to share his reproach will be ready and perhaps willing—yes, certainly willing—to participate in his glory. Only those can hear the concluding benediction of Hebrews and make any sense of it.

> Now the God of peace, that brought again from the dead our Lord Jesus, that great shepherd of the sheep, through the blood of the everlasting covenant, make you perfect in every good work to do his will, working in you that which is well-pleasing in his sight, through Jesus Christ; to whom be glory for ever and ever. Amen.

Notes

1. *Confessions*, Book III.

2. Lesslie Newbigin, *Sin and Salvation* (Philadelphia: Westminster Press, 1957), p. 19.

3. Second Inaugural Address.

4. *Confessions*, Book VIII.

5. Anselm, *Cur Deus Homo* (Chicago: Open Court Publishing Co., 1939), pp. 194-96, *passim.*

6. *Ibid.*, p. 196.

7. S. Kierkegaard, *Fear and Trembling* (Princeton: Princeton University Press, 1945), p. 28.

8. *Ibid.*, p. 26.

9. Karl Marx, *Communist Manifesto* (Chicago: Henry Regnery, 1954), pp. 23, 33.

10. *The Journal of the Rev. John Wesley, A.M.* (London: Epworth Press, 1938), I, pp. 475-76.

11. "The Passion of the Holy Martyrs Perpetua and Felicitas," in *The Ante-Nicene Fathers* (Buffalo, 1885), III, pp. 704-5.

12. C. S. Lewis, *Surprised by Joy* (New York: Harcourt, Brace, and Co., 1955), pp. 228-29.

13. John Donne, "Hymn to God My God, in my Sickness," in *John Donne* (Baltimore: Penguin Books, 1958), p. 178.

14. Amos N. Wilder, in *The Interpreter's Bible* (Nashville: Abingdon Press, 1957), XII, p. 224.

15. *Confessions*, Book II.

16. Wallace Stevens, "Sunday Morning," in Alan Swallow, ed.,

The Rinehart Book of Verse (New York: Rinehart & Co., Inc., 1952), p. 340.

17. See Oscar Cullmann's interesting discussion of the two witnesses in *Peter: Disciple, Apostle, Martyr* (Philadelphia: Westminster Press, 1953), pp. 88-89.

18. C. S. Lewis, *That Hideous Strength* (New York: The Macmillan Company, 1946).

19. Martin Rist, in *The Interpreter's Bible*, XII, pp. 414-15.

20. Sven Lidman, *På resan genom livet* (Stockholm, 1934), pp. 75-81.

Format by Katharine Sitterly
Set in Linotype Janson
Composed, printed and bound by The Haddon Craftsmen, Inc.
HARPER & ROW, PUBLISHERS, INCORPORATED